"This book offers an explicit, hai approach to the fundamentals an nuances of parenting. It is an essential handbook for families who seek greater intimacy and happiness together."

Eleanor Osborne
Editor, Parent, Teacher

"As a former high school principal, I wish I had *Loving Is Natural, Parenting Is Not: creating a value-centered family* as a resource for parent education programs and for helping parents with the difficult task of raising their children with positive values. This book is a valuable resource in a much neglected field."

Dr. Thomas M. Jones, Senior Associate
National Alliance for
Restructuring Education

"The authors have written this book with sensitivity, wisdom and practicality. Not only will it help train parents and educators in the art of parenting and in the promoting of *ValueSkills,* but it will act as a beacon for our children who, in turn, will become effective future parents."

Norma Laboy Bushorr
Parent and Principal

... parents to rediscover some of the simple gifts that first made 'family life' seem like such a good idea."

Margaret Cronin
Parent and Writer on Parent Issues

"This book helped me realize that it is never too late to make things better and to improve upon my relationship with my child."

Bernadette Canfield
Parent and Teacher

"'*Loving (your child) is Natural, Parenting Is Not*' offers sound advice, practical applications and lessens the feeling of isolation many parents experience."

Nan Westervelt, Executive Director
Young Audiences of Rochester

"One of the most invaluable gifts we can give to our children… *ValueSkills!* This book is packed with common sense guidance and practical activities to help build strong, healthy and loving relationships within our families."

Inta Grymin
Parent and Teacher

Books By Gil and Tanya Gockley

Loving Is Natural, Parenting Is Not:
creating a value-centered family
(Coleman Press)

Books By Gil Gockley

Classroom Super Teams: Becoming A Better Neighbor,
Books K, I and II, Illustrated by Sue Arnold
(Life/Career Education)

Classroom Super Teams: Responsibility Toward Self, Others,
Community, Books III, IV, V and VI
(Life/Career Education)

Career Insights and Self-Awareness Games
Gilbert Gockley and Harold Munson
(Houghton Mifflin)

Best wishes to you and your family
Gil and Tanya

Loving Is Natural, Parenting Is Not:

creating a value-centered family

Dr. Gil Gockley

Tanya Tihansky Gockley

Coleman Press

P.O. Box 92339

Rochester, New York 14692

Illustrations: Tanya Tihansky Gockley
Cover Design and Book Layout: Lisa Lange (Rochester, N.Y.)
Photograph of Gil and Tanya Gockley: Leichtner Studios (Rochester, N.Y.)

ISBN 0-9651889-0-6
SAN 298-9492
Library of Congress Catalog Number: 96-85939

Published in the United States of America

Coleman Press
P.O. Box 92339
Rochester, New York 14692
Telephone/Fax: 716.242.0688

Dedicated to our parents who gave us roots
and allowed us to grow and blossom:
Chas and Floretta Gockley
Theodore and June Tihansky

Dedicated to our treasured children and grandchildren:
Jared, Coleman, Christopher, Terri, Christopher and Casidhe

Dedicated to all individuals who experience
the journey of being a parent

Acknowledgments

The genesis for writing *Loving Is Natural, Parenting Is Not: creating a value-centered family* began in California with the support of Sally Marshall of Sally Marshall Talent, Inc. and Gar Smith and Robin Hirsch of Imagecraft, Inc. We are sincerely fortunate to have worked with these fine people.

There are many individuals who have encouraged us and touched our lives in our endeavor to make this book a reality. Our heartfelt appreciation is extended to family members, friends, parents, educators, community leaders and youth who have provided support and who share our dream of creating value-centered families. We thank those who have participated in our parenting seminars and family weekend retreats. We also want to thank our son, Jared, for the many hours he spent helping type our manuscript, to Lisa Lange of Lange Design for her patience and talent in laying out our book and designing our cover and to Nan Westervelt who stated 'loving your child is natural, parenting is not' in her book endorsement and allowed us to adapt it for our title.

We acknowledge the following individuals for their invaluable ideas, advice and support: Don and Bonnie Fox, A. Richard Barber, Paul Littrell, Eleanor Osborne, David Vitale, Greg Doyle, Rob Ford, Skip Hansford, Joe Grymin, Peg Cronin, Ted and Kathy Nixon, Paula Pilarski, Marilyn Stein, Lou Zona, Robert Kendall, Russ Lunn, Debbie Bellisario, Mimi Bisbee, Georgie Bramley, Caren Glassman, Barbara Roach, Sylvia Rowe, Carol Schacht, Ruth Telarico and Kathleen Winn.

We also acknowledge pioneers in the field of interpersonal communications who helped us realize the need to listen, to ask questions and to reflect feelings when interacting with our children: Rudolf Dreikurs, Haim Ginott, William Glasser and Thomas Gordon. We acknowledge David Krathwohl and associates who paved the way for a better understanding of the affective (internalization) process.

Table of Contents

Loving Is Natural, Parenting Is Not:
creating a value-centered family

Preface   i

Chapter 1: A New Beginning   1
  • Parenting Challenges   2

Chapter 2: Why We Stopped Teaching Values   7

Chapter 3: A Total Approach To Parenting   15

Chapter 4: Conducting Your Family Orchestra   29
  • Calmness: A Key To Communication   30
  • Parenting Skills   31
  • Team-building Skills   43

Chapter 5: Basic Communication Skills   49
  • The Issue of Ignoring   51
  • The Problem with Interrupting   52
  • The Necessity for Calmness   53
  • The Wonder of Listening   54
  • The Importance of Asking Clarifying Questions   55
  • The Power of Sending Direct Messages   56
  • The Gift of Validating Statements   59
  • The Significance of Self-affirming Statements   60
  • The Delicate Nature of Direct Command Statements   62

Chapter 6: Reward, Praise And Punishment
Versus Discipline With Calmness And Dignity   65

Chapter 7: Discipline With Calmness And Dignity 75
- Stage One: Teaching 76
- Stage Two: Talking 77
- Stage Three: Problem-solving 79
- Stage Four: Seeking Additional Support 85

Chapter 8: As A Parent, I Will Remember . . . 89
- Parenting Checklist 91

Chapter 9: Family Activities For Teaching *ValueSkills® I* 97
- Listening 102
- Friendliness 108
- Kindness 117
- Cooperation 123
- Encouragement 128
- Honesty (with Kindness) 134
- Patience 140

Chapter 10: Family Activities For Teaching *ValueSkills® II* 147
- Consideration 150
- Courtesy 156
- Respect for Property 161
- Responsibility for Personal Care 166
- Self-confidence 171
- Enthusiasm 178
- Courage 185

Glossary 192
Index 199
Ordering Information 202

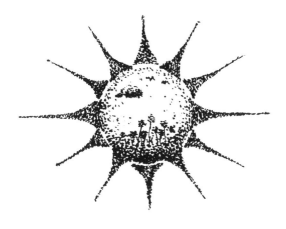

We must learn

to nurture

each of our family members

as if our future depends on it.

Because it does.

Preface

Loving our children is natural. Like parents everywhere, I remember the joy and hope I felt when the nurse laid my son in my arms for the first time. But 22 years later, cradling my son's son, I contemplated what a different world he was entering. Today's world is bombarded with the illegal use of drugs, the blare of music glorifying violence and the media sanctifying greed. It's a world in which, from Little League to the Olympics, winning has become more important than loving. Surrounding us is a world in which the gentle voices of respect and responsibility are too often over-shadowed by fear, anxiety, anger and indifference. Raising children in this world has become difficult and confusing and is not a natural process in which parents know just what to do. There are no easy answers and no guarantees. *Loving is natural, parenting is not.*

Yet I remain hopeful. The spark of hope comes not from the promise of school reforms or government sponsored programs. It glows not from some grandiose scheme, but from the hearts and homes of people like you and me. We love our children and want them to be of strong character. The hope for our children and for our country depends on our ability to teach them as well as future generations a few simple but powerful inner strengths. These strengths are called values.

Values were once strong in our society; today they've dimmed. We have the power to revive and restore them in our homes. Home is where the journey begins. Home is where the hope is.

This book is the result of my lifelong interest in a simple but vital question: "*What really matters?*" Although this question can generate hours of discussion, it all boils down to this: What really matters is the fullest possible flowering of human potential. To nurture this potential, we must learn to nurture each of our family members as if our future depends on it. Because it does.

This book presents the fruits of my quarter-century quest distilled into a practical set of ideas we can apply in our homes no matter how hectic and stress-filled our lives might be. These ideas can enrich our relationships with our children, regardless of the challenges we face as parents.

What this book offers are innovative methods for powerful, positive interactions between ourselves and our children. It offers a beacon of hope that shines brightly as respect, responsibility, dignity and integrity are reintroduced into our lives. It offers the sunlight that awakens the human spirit. Through this book, family harmony can flourish in your home. It is my gift to you. You, in turn, can make it your gift to your children.

Parents travel a

life-long journey

through

uncharted territory.

Chapter One

A New Beginning

As a young parent, I envisioned that parenting would bring countless moments of joy and thanksgiving, a sense of oneness and wholeness to my marriage and immeasurable wonder, splendor, and promise.

No one ever told me that parenting could be so time consuming and, sometimes, so painful and confusing. No one ever told me about the stress that parenting and family life could bring to marriage and family relationships.

But experience taught me that both joy and pain are an on-going part of parenting. Experience also taught me that there are approaches we can use to help prevent or lessen the impact of many of the problems families encounter. It taught me that there are positive and effective ways to deal with children.

Loving Is Natural, Parenting Is Not: creating a value-centered family provides hope and insight for those who explore the uncharted territory of parenting; it is a guide for traveling a path that has no crystal ball and no guarantee. It offers guidance and support for building family cohesiveness, even during difficult times. I encourage you to use the information about parenting and the family activities in this book to create a positive home environment where your family can live and grow, share and work together.

Parenting Challenges

The following parenting challenges serve as a foundation for dealing with children:

- to love children unconditionally
- to express feelings constructively
- to live "in the present"
- to set clear, firm, fair and consistent boundaries
- to make character development a priority

Love Children Unconditionally

The first challenge for us, as parents, is to give unconditional love to our children. It is as simple as saying and meaning, *"Although I may not like all of the things you say and do, I love you unconditionally. I love you without conditions."*

Consider these questions:

- Does your child feel you love her more when she wins than when she loses?
- Does your child feel you love him more when he earns A's than when he earns D's and E's?
- Does your child feel you love her more when she behaves according to your rules and moral beliefs?

If you answered "*yes*" to any of these questions, I encourage you to think about the messages you give your child. It is natural to feel pleased when your child wins contests, proud when your child receives A's, happy when your child behaves appropriately according to your standards and grateful when your child follows your moral principles and beliefs. But I suggest that your child needs to be 100% clear that you love him/her unconditionally and forever as a human being no matter what he/she does.

Express Feelings Constructively

We all have unique feelings about every situation. Feelings such as anger, sadness, joy and confusion, are neither right nor wrong. Feelings just are. We are better able to express ourselves appropriately to our children when we keep the focus on how we feel. In doing this we verbalize without judgments and put-downs. This means talking to children without accusing, blaming and name-calling, all of which result in feelings of resentment.

Think carefully as you read the statements listed below, noting that the speaker uses the pronoun "I" to show ownership when expressing constructively how he or she 'feels':

- "*I feel angry about what you did.* (appropriate response)" versus "*You make me so mad! How could you do this?* (inappropriate response)"

- "*I feel uncomfortable with what you just said.* (appropriate response)" versus "*You are a bad person for saying that!* (inappropriate response)"

- "*When you don't take your dishes into the kitchen after you finish watching TV, I feel disappointed. I expect you to assume responsibility for cleaning up after yourself.* (appropriate response)" versus "*You make a mess everywhere you go! You never clean up after yourself!* (inappropriate response)"

- "*I feel unhappy that your room is messy. When will you agree to clean it up?* (appropriate response)" versus "*Your room is a mess and you better get it cleaned up! Get in there and do it!* (inappropriate response)"

- "*I feel grateful that you decided to help me with the cleaning today.* (appropriate response)" versus "*It's about time you finally decided to help me clean the house.* (inappropriate response)"

Live In The Present

Today is a gift to all of us, that's why some people call it the "present." Many of us spend too much time complaining about what happened yesterday or planning for the future. While learning from the past and planning ahead are certainly necessary, it is a treasure to capture each moment. I believe two of the "golden gifts" we can give our spouses, our children and ourselves are listening to one another (really listening) and focusing on and living fully in the moment.

Set Boundaries

From the moment children are born, parents and children battle over boundaries, those often nebulous lines that separate acceptable behaviors from unacceptable behaviors. *The parent's job* is to create and maintain clear, fair boundaries (rules) for his or her child. *The child's job* is to challenge and extend boundaries in order to obtain greater personal freedom as he or she grows toward adulthood.

It is important that parents be clear about their expectations as they set and enforce reasonable and appropriate boundaries. When necessary, parents need to be comfortable using the word "*NO*" with their children.

So often parents feel alone when setting boundaries as other parents are unwilling to take a stand. They need to have courage to stand up for what they believe, to set rules and to follow through with them—even when their children wail "*But everyone else can do it!*" or "*Billy's mom doesn't make him do this!*" Children need guidance and support. Children need to know that parents are in charge so they can feel a sense of security.

To raise responsible children, adults need to be responsible parents.

Make Character Development A Priority

Character is defined as one's moral qualities and guiding principles. For the first 180 years of our country's history, schools, homes and community organizations taught basic common values, such as kindness, consideration, courtesy and cooperation; this led to the development of strong character in individuals. Over the last 40 years, these teachings seem to have practically disappeared from our social institutions.

Today, basic common values are not taught or even expected by many parents even though parents play an integral role in the development of character in their children. Parents need to identify the values and beliefs they feel are important, then teach and live those values and beliefs as honestly and fully as possible. As parents teach positive values and beliefs by example, they become beacons of light for their children.

The cry for *A New Beginning* that includes teaching children wholesome character traits is heard on talk radio as individuals express their frustrations and fears and through "time-to-change" editorials where concerned writers explore bold new ideas for solving societal problems. It is heard in national interviews that depict a frightened, unsettled citizenry screaming for security and order in their schools and on their streets. It is heard in political speeches made by men and women who know that our communities and country cannot stay economically viable if people continue to follow a path that is devoid of respect, responsibility and integrity. On such a path, fear overpowers love. "*Doing what I want at the expense of others*" replaces "*treating others as I want to be treated.*"

It is time for *A New Beginning*. The next chapter considers the events of the past 50 years that have brought us to the point where we, as a society, have stopped teaching basic common values.

As a society

many of us have stopped

respecting ourselves

and others,

stopped encouraging one another

and stopped caring.

Chapter Two

Why We Stopped Teaching Values

In the 1950s you knew where you stood. A friend of mine says that when he was ten years old he said the word *"Damn!"* outside the hardware store in his hometown. Not only did the store owner reprimand him, but by the time the youngster got home his parents were waiting; they already knew. Back then, the rules were known, the boundaries were clear. What's more, all of society's institutions—the school, the church, the neighborhood, even the hardware store owner joined in reinforcing those rules. The rules were based on right and wrong. As a kid, you knew where you stood.

Things were simpler then. Ike was in the White House; Ozzie and Harriet were on the new invention known as the TV, and of course, *Father Knew Best.* The family dinner and the Sunday drive thrived.

If kids stepped out of line—that invisible but universally recognized line—the heavy hand of authority loomed "as soon as your father gets home." Back then, not only did kids know where they stood, they also knew clearly who was in charge and what values, behaviors and conformities were expected. This authoritarian structure provided order.

Post-war wages, like families, grew; suburbia blossomed, and our homes became gardens of electronic gadgets. This was a time of tremendous economic growth. Neither the shadow of Sputnik nor the dimly-heard departure of U.S. "advisors" to a far-off land called Vietnam muffled the promise of prosperity and stability in our families. Adding to our optimism was the promise of Camelot, as the grandfatherly Eisenhower was eclipsed by the rising son: the vibrant, witty and youthful man from Massachusetts.

Taking the Presidential Oath of Office on a frigid January day, John F. Kennedy accepted the torch "passed to a new generation." The light from that torch cast a shadow over authoritarianism, and lit the path of change for America, a path that empowered the nation's youth to question much of what they inherited from the preceding generation. This path did not lead back to history, tradition and authority; it led young people, forward and inward, to their own power and potential as individuals. As the basic institutions and the autocratic structures in our society were challenged, the cry for individual rights—women, minority groups, children, even animal rights—was heard across the nation.

People began looking beyond autocratic corporate America in an effort to explore the meaning and purpose of life. The 1960s presented many opportunities for self-discovery. Attending graduate school during this period of time, I found myself in the middle of what was dubbed "the human potential movement." This movement encouraged individuals to break from the lockstep, authoritarian rigidity of the 1950s. Self-actualization became the watchword. People began encountering their inner beings and discovering new levels of awareness. This path of change energized a generation. But eventually this path took an unexpected turn toward self-centeredness.

If the importance of each individual was to be realized through self-discovery, and if individuals no longer looked to authorities for answers, then how was society to impart its values to its citizens?

Schools replaced "teaching" values with "clarifying" them. In the 1970s, public educators decided that their role would be to aid in this self-discovery process.

In the process of trying to be sensitive to the "rights" of all people, educators tried not to impose or even expose values onto students. No longer was it clear what values, if any, could be promoted in the schools. Helping students discover their own values became the goal. Without teaching core values in classrooms across the country, it was a puzzling time.

Unfortunately, homes became equally confusing and ambiguous places for children. As values disappeared, family relationships began to crumble.

Without teaching the guiding principles upon which this country was founded, how could children be expected to assimilate them? Even though basic values were no longer taught in the schools, children continued to be exposed to values through other sources, especially media and music.

In homes during the 1970s, children were exposed to a powerful new influence—the television. They became susceptible to TV's messages about everything, from fashions to breakfast cereals. What they saw, they wanted; what they wanted, they demanded. And many parents said yes.

Parents said yes partly because they could afford to, since many families had dual incomes, but they also said yes because they simply wanted to provide more for their children. They justified that their dual incomes would provide a better life for them. And they were told by the "experts" that what mattered was not the amount of time spent with their kids but the "quality" of that time. Nevertheless, kids and parents began realizing that their home life and relationships didn't quite match that of the *Brady Bunch.*

These baby boom parents were creating competition in the work force while the economy began moving toward recession. Educators began publishing and comparing students' annual reading and math achievement test scores, which brought about increased competition in the schools. This prompted an immediate shift from child-centered to subject-centered education in order to improve test scores. At this point, the only thing that seemed to matter to most teachers and parents was achievement. Better grades, higher test scores and a greater quality of academic performance became our national priorities.

For this reason, during the 1980s, our country, particularly our educational system, adopted a purely behavioral approach to education. This approach called for developing and teaching measurable objectives. The catch phrase of the day was "to create 'effective schools' and get 'back to the basics.' " In doing this, the importance of values was diminished. Since a child's character cannot be so easily quantified, moral and ethical growth—in short, values—dropped out of the schools' curriculum.

By the end of the decade we had neutralized our national values system and America felt a void. Those who could, escaped through the excesses of the 1980s. We filled our closets with the "right" clothes, filled our homes with "order-before-midnight-tonight" gadgets, and filled our leisure time with self-fulfillment activities. No matter how large these diversions were, they were never large enough to fill the void. Something was missing. Something intangible. Something inside.

In trying to organize the perfect life without damaging what the "experts" told us were our children's sensitive and vulnerable self-images, everything we gave them was overshadowed by the implications of what we failed to give them: the basic values for sculpting a meaningful life. During the spring of 1988, a lovely high school senior came to me in tears and said, "*I'm doing everything that's asked of me. I get all A's and B's, my college board scores are great, I'm with the popular kids, I play varsity sports and I even have a part-time job! Why do I feel so empty? Why don't I feel joy?*"

10

This young lady made me think about our efforts to fill our lives with a frenetic array of external activities without a context of internal values. Achievement, being popular and winning at sports put tremendous pressure on children. We lost perspective and balance in our homes and schools. For too many of our children, home and school became overwhelming, even devastating experiences.

Ever since the "back to basics" movement began in the early 1980s, educators also felt increasing pressure to produce tangible and measurable results. In such an environment, numbers—grades, achievement scores and team win/loss records—are daily measures of success. Children learn that these numbers are too often the only things that really count. As a result, they accept the "winning is everything, so win at any cost" philosophy that they see all around them in professional sports, in the business world and in politics.

The lack of teaching our children values has brought attention to other numbers, the ones we read in our daily newspapers. These include the number of dropouts, the number of teen pregnancies and the number of drug and alcohol related deaths among our youth. What about the number of teen suicides? Or the number of youngsters who use violence as a form of self-expression? Or the number of assaults on our streets and in our schools? Or the number of business owners who cannot find employees who have an understanding of or a commitment to the kind of work ethic that helped build this country?

We all continue to pay a heavy price for these numbers. The price is paid in lost productivity, but more importantly, it is paid in lost humanity. Can we really afford to build jails and rehab centers to take care of a responsibility that we have for so long neglected? Can we really afford to live in fear of the very people who represent the future of this country? Can we really afford to sit back and wait for politicians and policemen and lawyers and teachers to take on the tasks which we, as parents, can do better, more efficiently and more effectively? In other words, can we really afford to lose one more generation of American youth? For unless we can find a different approach, that is exactly what will happen.

A new approach to respect, responsibility, dignity and integrity cannot follow the path of the last 40 years. The strict authoritarianism of the 1950s is not the answer. Nor is the "do your own thing" approach of the 1960s. We've awakened to the price America has paid for the self-absorption of the 1970's "me" generation. And we have become painfully aware that among the so-called basics that the 1980's "Back-to-basics" movement has not produced are the basic attitudes and behaviors, the values and the character that we want to see in our politicians, our business leaders, our neighbors, our children and ourselves.

As a society many of us have stopped respecting ourselves and others, stopped talking to each other, stopped encouraging one another and stopped caring. For the past 40 years, we have not adequately dealt with the task of helping children internalize and develop moral character. Parents, educators and community leaders need to re-focus their priorities and combine their efforts to develop personal and social responsibility, as well as a sense of well being in our children. Parents are the key to beginning this process of change.

The premise of this book is that we, as parents, have the power to make a difference. We can choose to travel along a path leading to our children's development of respect and moral character. This is a path to growth—ours as well as our children's. It is a path of opportunity and hope. It is a path to harmony in our homes.

50-Year Historical Perspective On Why We Stopped Teaching Values:

1950s - focus on history, tradition, order and authority
- rules were clear—based on right and wrong
- "you knew where you stood"
- values were taught and expected

1960s - focus on human rights
- youth were empowered to question past ideas and traditions
- "do your own thing"
- all values were questioned

1970s - focus on self-discovery
- youth no longer looked to authorities for answers—society no longer imparted its values to its citizens
- "the me generation"
- values were no longer taught—children were asked to clarify their own values

1980s - focus on measurable results—achievement and productivity
- a time of diversions—exercise, material possessions and self-fulfilling activities
- "winning at any cost—self-centeredness"
- something was missing/something intangible/something inside — values were missing

1990s - focus on change
- national statistics reflect not only a loss in productivity but also in humanity
- "the development of values and moral character"
- parents, educators and community leaders begin teaching and modeling basic common values

A total approach
to parenting

calmness

parenting skills

team-building
skills

communication skills

discipline with
calmness and dignity

teaching and modeling
the 14 ValueSkills

Leads to:
Dignity, Hope, Respect, Responsibility

Chapter Three

A Total Approach To Parenting

Parenting is a journey. A Chinese proverb by Lao Tzu says that a journey of a thousand miles must begin with a single step. By reading this book, you are joining me in taking one of these vital steps. This book presents a total approach to parenting that guides us along a path filled with more hope than we experience in our world today. It guides us along a path providing opportunities to acquire the dignity and integrity necessary for all parents and children to become enriched and fully human.

This chapter provides an overview of the parenting approach presented in *Loving Is Natural, Parenting Is Not*. Several paths converge to create this approach that leads to dignity, hope, respect, and responsibility (see figure on opposite page).

This approach begins with a path that challenges us to develop calmness within ourselves as we interact with others and to enhance our capacity to remain in control, particularly during times of stress and conflict.

It also introduces parenting skills that prompt us to examine our own personal approach to parenting. These skills are essential guidelines for dealing with children. Following these guidelines makes parenting more enjoyable and less stressful, allowing us to be more fulfilled in our role as parents.

An additional path shows us how to develop a family team through the support and encouragement of family members, enabling us to comfort them and restore hope when necessary. Being part of a family team provides a sense of security, worth and belonging to every family member.

Creating a family team requires effective communication. *Loving Is Natural, Parenting Is Not* includes communication activities that enhance our abilities to listen to and understand each other, and to express ourselves appropriately. It prepares us to put common sense communication skills into common practice.

The initial skills and strategies presented in this book foster calmness, respect and dignity between parents and children. They are the foundation of an innovative approach to disciplining children. This new discipline approach, called *Discipline with Calmness and Dignity,* is presented in Chapter Seven. It teaches children what is expected, encourages parents to identify behaviors that are inappropriate and redirects misbehavior through dialogue and problem-solving. It urges families to seek additional support when they need help. Families become stronger as parents choose, promote and model the attitudes and behaviors they would like to see in themselves and in their children.

Since 1970, my experiences with children and young adults have taught me that, in most instances, misbehaviors relate to a lack of respect, responsibility and good citizenship. My experiences have also taught me that to understand the meaning of these qualities, children need to first be awakened to more basic values. This book identifies 14 basic values as inner strengths called *ValueSkills®*.

ValueSkills include:

ValueSkills® I
1. listening
2. friendliness
3. kindness
4. cooperation
5. encouragement
6. honesty
   (with kindness)
7. patience

ValueSkills® II
8. consideration
9. courtesy
10. respect
    for property
11. responsibility
    for personal care
12. self-confidence
13. enthusiasm
14. courage

Children must first be made aware of these *ValueSkills* before they can start transforming the idea of values into practical skills and behaviors.

Values are internal beliefs.

Skills are practical behaviors that can be taught, practiced and improved.

ValueSkills® are essential, common inner strengths, basic character traits (values), that can be identified, taught and modeled (skills), and, that serve as the foundation for character development.

Asking "*What are ValueSkills?*" is different than asking, "*What things do I value?*" What we value relative to material possessions varies widely. *ValueSkills,* on the other hand, are universally held beliefs that most people, regardless of income, race, religion or national origin agree upon.

During the course of my work with young adults, teachers, parents and community leaders, these 14 *ValueSkills* have been identified by using a time-proven test. The test to identify values that are common to all people asks one simple question:

What are the qualities and character traits you would like to see in ...
> . . . your spouse,
> . . . your children,
> . . . your neighbors,
> . . . your friends,
> . . . your colleagues, and
> . . . your boss?

Please complete the following sentence: "*I would like my spouse, children, neighbors, friends, colleagues and boss to be (more) _____.*"

Through the years, this time-proven test has continued to yield similar answers. These common answers became *ValueSkills*. The second half of this book includes family activities for teaching these *ValueSkills* to children.

As we teach and model the 14 *ValueSkills*, our children internalize values which guide their behaviors. Ultimately each of them develops an internal value system, an individual system of interests, appreciations, values and beliefs based on their experiences. As children are introduced to *ValueSkills* they are more likely to choose to act in a respectful and responsible manner. *ValueSkills* become a natural part of their character. *ValueSkills* become the voice of their behavior, a voice that speaks things like "I know what it is to be friendly and I like it when people treat me in a friendly manner, so I choose to treat others this way."

Children often need to observe *ValueSkills* being modeled before putting them into action. That modeling is up to us. Unfortunately there is also a need for us to pause and reflect on the conflicting and negative messages that bombard our children everyday. We are not our children's only teachers. They are like sponges, absorbing information from many sources – the media, peers and society in general. And, there is sadly a need for caution as children relate to and interact with others.

While being interviewed on the radio several years ago, a concerned father called the station asking, "*What about Stranger Danger? How can we teach children to be friendly, kind and cooperative when this behavior could be a problem in certain situations? I don't want my child to be the victim of a stranger.*" It is important to find a balance between teaching children to use *ValueSkills* that build relationships with significant people in their lives, and being cautious in their behaviors with strangers. There must be a difference between how we respond to strangers and how we respond to family members. We need to teach, model and practice common sense and discretion regarding the use of any of the 14 *ValueSkills,* just as we practice common sense and discretion in other areas of our lives.

"*How do we want to treat our spouses, children and neighbors?*" "*How do we want others, especially people we care about, to treat us?*" When we answer these questions, it is clear that *ValueSkills* need to become our standards for behavior. They provide the practical skills necessary to act upon the "Golden Rule": *Treat others the way you want to be treated.*

Being kind because we believe in kindness (*ValueSkill*) and being kind because we might "get something out of it" are two different forms of motivation. We can be kind to the boss hoping to get a raise or a promotion or perhaps because in doing so we think she might overlook the fact that we ducked out of work early yesterday. In these cases, we act kindly, but our motivation is the hope of reward or fear of punishment. Therefore the kindness is not genuine.

A value needs to be internalized before it becomes genuine. This means that it needs to become part of a person's belief system. To develop behavior that is genuine, we need to go through a process of value creation that moves from simply being aware of a value to truly living the value.

Becoming aware of a value involves being open minded and

willing to explore its definitions and benefits. We then move from simply talking about the value to actually using it in our behavior. When we begin to use it in our behavior, without the promise of reward or threat of punishment, we are personally choosing to live the value.

We begin to feel an internal spark of energy within ourselves and experience emotional satisfaction. The moment we feel emotionally good about acting in accordance with a specific value, we have tentatively acquired the value.

As we use the value more often and it becomes the behavior that we prefer to use, our initial spark of energy becomes a torch lighting the way. As the value is fully internalized it becomes an essential part of our character, and we now are committed to using it each day.

Each of the 14 *ValueSkills* can be internalized in this manner. *ValueSkills* become brilliant lights of guiding energy as we genuinely internalize and live each one of them.

When this process of internalization has taken place, we are able to affirm *ValueSkills* to ourselves and others. We act in accordance with what we believe and how we see ourselves. *We prove every day who we think we are.* For example, if we believe we are kind we act in a kind manner. The process of value creation helps each of us become happier, more authentic and more contributing family members. The activities in Chapters Nine and Ten are designed to help bring about the internalization of the 14 *ValueSkills*. Experiencing these activites with children increases awareness of these common values and clarifies their definitions and benefits.

Visualize our homes, our children's classrooms, our schools, our places of employment and our community organizations where a majority of people act upon the first seven *ValueSkills:*

Visualize our homes

where each family member says,

"I am a calm person,

a good listener, friendly,

kind, cooperative, encouraging,

honest (with kindness)

and patient."

listening

friendliness

kindness

cooperation

encouragement

honesty (with kindness)

patience

It is the internalization and interaction of these first seven *ValueSkills I* that start a process that genuinely helps people to:

- enhance their sense of security, worth and belonging,
- treat others with respect and dignity,
- attain personal and social responsibility, and
- act and choose with integrity.

ValueSkills I character traits are prerequisites for developing the second set of character traits, *ValueSkills II* listed below:

consideration

courtesy

respect for property

responsibility for personal care

self-confidence

enthusiasm

courage

Now, visualize our homes, our children's classrooms, our schools, our places of employment and our community organizations where a majority of people say to themselves, *"Not only am I a good listener, I am friendly, I am kind, I am cooperative, I am encouraging, I am honest (with kindness) and I am patient, but I am also considerate, I am courteous, I am respectful of property, I am responsible for personal care, I am self-confident, I am enthusiastic and I am courageous."*

The awareness and internalization of these 14 *ValueSkills* form the framework for building strong character. When firmly in place, this foundation supports a series of additional values, attitudes and

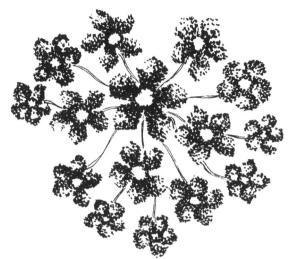

Now visualize our homes

where each family member says,

not only, "I am a calm person,

a good listener, friendly,

kind, cooperative, encouraging,

honest (with kindness) and patient,"

but also "I am considerate,

courteous, respectful of property,

responsible for personal care,

self-confident, enthusiastic and courageous."

behaviors such as thoughtfulness, appreciation, curiosity, helpfulness, caring and generosity. Ultimately, a values complex—an internalized set of interconnected values and virtues—begins to develop. A healthy internal values complex leads to actions of respect, responsibility and good citizenship.

- *Being respectful* of others demonstrates a trust that every human being has worth and significance and deserves to be treated with dignity.
- *Being responsible* demonstrates accountability for one's behaviors and duties.
- *Being a good citizen* demonstrates participation in good faith in the affairs of one's community and country.

As we develop an internal values complex, we begin to form a set of virtues, defined as qualities of character that guide each of us to respond and choose in an honorable manner, even when we have no audience. Some common virtues that we internalize and act upon include:

Loyalty: The quality of maintaining one's obligations and commitments to those with whom one has relationships

Trust: The quality of believing in others who demonstrate a sense of honor and integrity

Good Will: The quality of finding goodness in people and in life

Self-control: The quality of seeking balance in one's life; of being "in control" of one's behavior

Self-reliance: The quality of having the self-confidence and courage to give one's best effort in completing tasks and solving problems

Discretion: The quality of making prudent and wise decisions and choices

Endurance: The quality of being patient and persistent; having the courage and inner strength to continue

Moral Strength: The quality of acting upon that which is ethical in order to maintain the principles of humanity

A values complex,

an internalized set of

interconnected values and virtues,

leads to actions of respect,

responsibility and good citizenship.

Justice: The quality of being fair and equitable toward ourselves and
others

Due Process: The quality of providing equal application of the law
and a fair hearing to all members of society

Now, visualize our homes, our children's classrooms, our
schools, our places of employment and our community organizations where a majority of people say to themselves not only . . .

" *I am a good listener,*
I am friendly,
I am kind,
I am cooperative,
I am encouraging,
I am honest (with kindness),
I am patient,
I am considerate,
I am courteous,
I am respectful of property,
I am responsible for personal care,
I am self-confident,
I am enthusiastic and
I am courageous, but also . . .
I am thoughtful,
I am appreciative,
I am curious,
I am helpful,
I am caring,
I am generous,
I am respectful of others,
I am responsible,
I am a good citizen,
I am loyal,
I am trustworthy,

I am a person of good will,
I am a person with self-control,
I am self-reliant,
I am discreet,
I am a person who has endurance,
I am a person of moral strength,
I am just, and
I am fair regarding equal application of the law."

The items on this list are more than a collection of *ValueSkills* and virtues. They are the signposts of a civilized society. They are the signposts of individuals exhibiting healthy character, defined as moral integrity. If the majority of us lived in accordance with them, our country, our communities, our relationships and our lives would be richer and more joyful.

These signposts of civilization point us toward that joy. They point in a direction that fosters respect, responsibility, dignity and integrity. They lead to caring in our communities, to security on our streets, and most of all, to harmony in our homes.

The skills and attitudes

you develop in your child

through this parenting approach

will echo into

the next generation.

Chapter Four

Conducting Your Family Orchestra

Over the years, watching Arthur Fiedler conduct the Boston Pops Orchestra has been an inspiration. Here was a man who brought together a group of creative, talented and diverse individuals and saw to it that each of these musicians had something unique to contribute to the whole. When the maestro raised his baton, these individuals came together in a common purpose. What emerged was magic as well as music, and it is that magic that fills me with excitement as I present this parenting approach to you.

You are your family's conductor; they are your orchestra. Neither you nor anyone in your household can compose a concert if each of you remains a soloist. What would be missing is the harmony, the magic of the whole being greater than any of the individual parts.

Like any orchestra, your family consists of creative, talented and diverse individuals. Your job as conductor is to develop positive attitudes, that when properly mixed, will score the symphony entitled

Harmony At Home.

My goal is to empower you as the conductor of your family's orchestra. You can wield your baton with the firm but gentle motion of a maestro as you practice the attitudes and actions required for positive parenting.

Arthur Fiedler's spirit remains part of the Boston Pops, even though the baton has passed to another conductor. The music and the magic continue to bear his mark. In the same manner, the skills and attitudes you develop in your children through this parenting approach will echo into the next generation. It will be your legacy: the music and the magic that naturally emerge from your efforts.

So, maestro, let your family's symphony begin.

Calmness: A Key To Communication

Have you ever noticed that musicians pause when a conductor steps on stage? No matter how intense their music will be, they always set aside a moment of quiet before letting their instruments speak. That moment of calmness is a key element of their success.

Calmness is also a key element in parenting, teaching and learning, each requiring an atmosphere that is similar to that moment of tranquillity before a concert begins. Whatever term we choose to call it—calmness, gentleness, composure or quietness—this special condition is important for listening effectively to one another.

If we are to really hear information being presented to us, we need to hear with all of our senses. We need to train ourselves to stop doing more than one thing at a time so that we can listen effectively. Listening for understanding takes total concentration. It requires hearing information without judgment. We need to listen not only to the words, but to the feelings behind the words. To do this, we need to gain the composure that calmness grants us. Hearing our children's feelings and thoughts is difficult to do in our hectic and stress-filled lives without first establishing a calm atmosphere.

Calmness gives us an edge when interacting with our children.

It is necessary to create a sense of calmness within ourselves so that we not only can be in control of our behavior, but can also be aware of our feelings. Only when we model calmness can we ask it of our children.

It is possible to create "moments of calmness" with our children by asking them to get comfortable and sit quietly for 10-15 seconds. It may be helpful for them to slowly breathe in and out a few times. Initially, children may find this difficult to do. Be patient. After practicing sitting calmly several times, children do it naturally and with ease. When parents and children practice calmness, it creates an environment for responding thoughtfully rather than impulsively to situations. Our intent is not to shut down spontaneous spirit but to create an atmosphere in which a parent and child can respond in constructive ways.

Calmness helps generate positive feelings and thoughts.
Positive feelings and thoughts help yield positive behaviors.
Positive behaviors help develop positive attitudes.
As we focus on the positive, we begin to find goodness in others.
We begin catching our children doing things right.
Calmness is one of the key skills we need for constructive parenting.

Parenting Skills

Parenting is often a challenging process of split-second decision-making, compromising and second-guessing. It can be an agonizing cycle of setting-up rules, expecting compliance, experiencing child resistance, fighting and giving in. This cycle causes us to act inconsistently and brings about confusion for everyone.

When fluctuating between being an autocratic parent and a permissive parent, we move from yelling and threatening our children at one moment to ignoring or pampering them the next. We find ourselves moving from one extreme to another: from the overreacting, overly-critical demanding parent to the overprotective, rescuing and overly-accommodating parent. Such extremes drain our energy and take the enjoyment out of parenting.

We need to find ways to make parenting less stressful, more pleasurable and more consistent. We begin by looking at the following ten parenting skills. Most of them are familiar. What's new is their power when used in combination with each other:

- Stay Calm
- Listen
- Encourage
- Use *ValueSkills*®
- Give Appropriate Attention
- Give Appropriate Responses
- Explain
- Allow for Compromise
- Allow for Consequences
- Apologize

The following pages highlight the ten parenting skills, presenting helpful information that can be used immediately. I encourage you to refer to these pages often.

Stay Calm

Speak calmly to your child.

Control your temper.

Take time-out to keep your cool.

Talk things out calmly instead of attacking.

Avoid name-calling and saying damaging things.

Never verbally abuse your child.

Never physically abuse your child.

Listen

Listen to your child.

Learn not to lecture, criticize and threaten.

Identify the concern being expressed.

Interrupting keeps you from hearing what your child is saying.

Show that you care through listening.

Sort out feelings without over-reacting to words or actions.

Treat your child with respect.

Teach your child good listening skills.

Establish an atmosphere of calmness.

Enhance your ability to listen by using the 14 ValueSkills.

Notice your child's facial expressions and body language.

Nobody likes being dominated or interrogated.

Encourage

Encouragement:

> *means inspiring, loving,*
> *reassuring, supporting and*
> *believing in someone,*
>
> *results in internal motivation,*
>
> *is non-judgmental,*
>
> *is a form of cheerleading,*
>
> *means expressing*
> *appreciation*
> *for effort,*
>
> *focuses on the positive, and*
>
> *acknowledges your*
> *child's strengths.*

Use ValueSkills®

ValueSkills are the roots of character.

Model ValueSkills to your child.

Teach ValueSkills to your child.

kindness ❖ *honesty (with kindness)* ❖ *encouragement*
enthusiasm ❖ *cooperation* ❖ *patience* ❖ *good listening*
friendliness ❖ *consideration* ❖ *self-confidence*
respect for property ❖ *courage* ❖ *courtesy*
responsibility for personal care

Give Appropriate Attention

Talk with and listen to your child.

Spend time with your child – enjoying activities which strengthen your relationship.

Catch your child doing positive things and reinforce these behaviors.

Teach your child the "Golden Rule."

Use humor to lighten up a situation.

Give Appropriate Responses

Increase positive talk.

*Share your feelings and thoughts
with honesty and kindness.*

*Give yourself time to think
before responding.*

*Express clearly what you expect
from your child.*

*Respond with respect
and encouragement.*

*Respond decisively, calmly
and consistently.*

*Give responses that do not put down
another person.*

*Portray an attitude that each problem
can and will be solved.*

Explain

*When your child asks or when you think it is
necessary, explain your position
clearly and briefly.*

Explain Clearly and Briefly

Allow for Compromise

Be open to exploring options.

Acknowledge your child's ideas.

Seriously consider other points of view.

*Recognize that there is more than one way
to solve a problem.*

*Don't control the situation by being
unnecessarily unyielding.*

*Consider working together to
find a third alternative
when you and your child don't agree.*

Allow for Consequences

Consequences provide valuable life lessons.

*Your child needs
to learn
the reality of 'cause and effect'
through experiencing safe consequences.*

*As a parent be
both firm and loving.*

*When necessary assume responsibility
for determining 'appropriate and reasonable'
consequences which relate to
your child's misbehavior.*

*As a parent, determine
who should assume responsibility
for solving the problem —
when it involves you,
become involved in finding solutions
and when it does not involve you,
encourage your child to assume responsibility
for solving the problem.*

Apologize

When appropriate say,

"I'm sorry"

(truly from the heart).

Being able to apologize

shows you have

strong character

and respect for your child.

Team-building Skills

Using the 10 parenting skills is important for building a family team. Creating a family team is like putting a puzzle together. A family needs all of the pieces in place to feel a sense of well-being. Consider that each family member has 14 basic puzzle pieces representing the 14 *ValueSkills*. A family with five members would have a family puzzle made up of 70 puzzle pieces. Yes, 70! With just one piece missing, the puzzle is incomplete. Every family member needs to be accountable for his or her own pieces. If one person chooses not to use one of the 14 *ValueSkills*, such as cooperation, the family cannot function effectively as a team. This shows how easily a family can lose its sense of harmony.

When a growing family consciously chooses to act in accordance with *ValueSkills*, each part of the whole (each family member) begins to build a philosophy of life based upon common inner strengths. As a result, the whole (the family) becomes stronger than the sum of the parts (each family member). The family becomes more cohesive and more supportive than ever before. *ValueSkills* provide a family with a sense of security, worth and belonging. Practicing *ValueSkills* creates a vital, effective family team.

Family cohesiveness becomes a reality when it is a goal and a priority. It is most easily attainable when parents begin to focus on building family unity early in each of their children's lives, although it is never too late to begin. We need to make good use of opportunities for guiding and encouraging our children to do their best, as well as to offer renewed hope when they feel discouraged.

As a parent . . .
- stress the positive—focus on the good,
- choose language that provides specific rather than general statements (*"I like the way you put your games away"* is more specific than *"I like the way you help around the house."*), and

- acknowledge your child's effort gently, honestly and kindly.

Working as a team brings about the magic of synergy, which is combining the energy and knowledge of two or more people to reach a common goal.

The following five components help to develop a solid family team:

Promoting

Promote *ValueSkills* by doing the family activities in Chapters Nine and Ten. Be alert to situations that provide opportunities to observe and discuss *ValueSkills* being practiced in your world. Talk about them. Discuss why *ValueSkills* are important in each circumstance. *ValueSkills* are the behaviors we expect from each other.

Modeling

If you teach and promote *ValueSkills,* you also need to live them. If you live them, your children will live them! Modeling each of the 14 *ValueSkills* is essential; after all, children learn more from what you do than from what you say. There are times when you'll blow it. When this happens, remember that no one is perfect. Forgive yourself, apologize when appropriate, and get on with the important tasks of parenting.

Cheerleading

Cheerleading is a form of encouragement. It is an enthusiastic and upbeat approach to creating family unity. Cheerleading can involve using the *ValueSkills* terms with your children in real-life situations:

- *"I appreciate when you treat your brother in a friendly manner. It makes our home a pleasant place to live."*
- *"Our family is really cooperating. Look at what we have accom-*

plished today."

A cheerleader gives positive comments, shows appreciation and applauds good effort.

When things are going well for your family—*celebrate.*

Unconditional Love

Loving each member of your family unconditionally, even during difficult times, is essential for creating harmony at home. Saying, "*You know that I love you even though I do not like what you just said (did),*" places the focus on the behavior and not on the person. We all need to know that we are loved by others even when our behaviors are unacceptable.

Goal-setting

Goal-setting is a key component of team-building. Working together toward the attainment of a goal enhances family cooperation. Goal-setting involves choosing a goal and deciding what action steps to take in order to achieve it. Goals can involve the entire family working together on a family goal or helping one family member to reach an individual goal.

Step One: Identify a goal and the timeline for completing the goal.
Examples:
- "*We will clean the garage on Saturday.*"
- "*I will wash the dishes five out of seven days a week during the month of October.*"
- "*I will write a letter to my grandparents by the end of the week.*"
- "*We will plant a garden by the end of May.*"
- "*I will be friendlier and more cooperative for the next 30 days.*"
- "*We will all be better listeners during this month.*"
- "*I will have the courage to say 'No' during this school year when my friends try to involve me in activities that, in my opinion, are*

inappropriate."

- "*We will eat together as a family at least five days a week for the next month.*"
- "*I will be kinder and more considerate to my younger sister during the next two weeks.*"

Step Two: Brainstorm ideas for reaching the goal, choose which idea(s) you want to use and put the idea(s) into practice. Be as specific as possible. Ask family members for suggestions.

Examples of ways a sibling could be kinder and more considerate to a younger sister during the next two weeks might include:

- reading a book to her,
- asking her to participate in an activity,
- playing a game with her,
- taking her to the store,
- inviting her to go to a movie,
- helping her with her homework,
- saying "please" and "thank you" to her, and
- smiling and saying "I love you."

Step Three: Evaluate your success in reaching the goal after putting the idea(s) into practice. As a part of team-building, it is important to meet with family members to discuss the successes and frustrations experienced while attempting to reach the goal.

The discussion(s) might include answering the following questions:

- Was the goal accomplished?
- Was it a difficult goal to attain?
- Did other people help you work toward reaching the goal?
- What feelings and thoughts describe the experience?
- Are additional brainstorming ideas necessary to help in reaching the goal?

A Goal-setting Guide

Name: _____ Date: _____

1. Write an Individual or Family Goal
   (include a date for the completion of the goal): _____

   _____

   _____

2. Brainstorm ideas that can help you reach the goal
   and place an "X" in front of the chosen suggestion(s):

   ___/ _____

   ___/ _____

   ___/ _____

   ___/ _____

   ___/ _____

3. Identify people who can help you reach the goal:

   _____

   _____

4. Write evaluations on your progress in reaching the goal:

   _____

   _____

   _____

   _____

When your family works as a team, everyone is a winner. Unlike professional sports teams, you don't need fancy equipment, a stand full of fans and a giant coliseum. For your family team, victories—even small, daily ones—are recorded not on the scoreboard of a stadium, but in the hearts of every family member.

We can record

positive images

of ourselves

in the hearts

of those we love.

Chapter Five

Basic Communication Skills

There is an old story about a young wife who made a practice of cutting a few inches off the end of a roast before putting it into the roasting pan. Periodically her husband would question her about why she did this. "*That's what you do with a roast,*" she would say. One day her mother observed her doing this and asked, "*Why are you cutting off the end of the roast?*" "*I can't believe you are asking me that,*" replied her daughter. "*I watched you cut off the ends of roasts for years.*" "*Oh, Honey,*" said the mother, "*I did that when the roasts were too large for my roasting pan.*"

This simple story reveals something we all do: misinterpret what we see and hear. The consequences of such miscommunication can range from a chuckle to hurt feelings to a disaster. When communication "hits the mark," trust, understanding and expected results emerge. When it "misses the mark," mistrust, ambiguity and unexpected results usually follow.

The intent of this chapter is to help individuals better understand one another. Having the skills to communicate effectively in our homes, particularly during times of stress, is necessary for building positive relationships. Many adults and children have used

49

the following step-by-step experiential approach to learn communication skills. I urge you to try these activities with your family.

Although a group experience is recommended, the activities can be studied by an individual without the benefit of a group experience.

Preparing for the Communication Activities

1. A group of people getting together to do these activities could include Mother, Dad, children, grandparents, relatives and friends.
2. Choose someone to read the directions for each activity.
3. Provide a timer to determine the ending point for each activity.
4. Each person chooses a partner.
5. The partners sit on chairs (or on pillows on the floor) facing each other. If the group has four people, there will be two rows of two people facing each other. If there is an uneven number of people, individuals take turns being an observer. Change partners after each activity so that everyone has an opportunity to work with several people.

There are nine communication activities in this chapter. As you experience them, remember to be helpful and patient with young children so they do not become overwhelmed or feel embarrassed.

Activity #1: The Issue of Ignoring

1. As a group, discuss what it means to ignore someone who is speaking. Possible discussion responses:
   * Ignoring is when you don't listen to another person.
   * Ignoring is when you don't pay attention to another person.
   * Ignoring is when you don't respond to another person.

2. Facing your partner, decide who will be Person A and who will be Person B.

3. A tells B about a favorite hobby or sports activity. B ignores A (60 seconds or less).

4. Repeat the same activity but reverse the roles.

5. As a group, answer the following question: "*What did you feel and think when you were ignored?*"

6. As a group, answer the following question: "*What did you feel and think when you ignored your partner?*"

Activity #2: The Problem with Interrupting

1. Change partners if there are more than two people.
2. As a group, discuss what it means to interrupt someone who is speaking. Possible discussion responses:
   - Interrupting is when you speak while another person is speaking.
   - Interrupting is when you make noise while another person is speaking.
   - Interrupting is when you break into a conversation between two other people.
3. Facing your partner, decide who will be Person A and who will be Person B.
4. A tells B about a favorite television show.
   B interrupts A several times (60 seconds or less).
5. Repeat the same activity but reverse the roles.
6. As a group, answer the following question: "*What did you feel and think when you were interrupted?*"
7. As a group, answer the following question: "*What did you feel and think when you interrupted your partner?*"

Activity #3: The Necessity for Calmness

1. Change partners if there are more than two people.
2. As a group, discuss what it means to be quiet and feel calm when being with someone. Possible discussion responses:
   • Calmness is sitting quietly.
   • Taking deep breaths helps a person feel more calm.
   • Calmness is the absence of agitation and excitement.
   • A calm person is better able to listen to another person.
   • It is easier to talk with a calm person.
3. Facing your partner, sit quietly and calmly for 30 seconds. It is not necessary to look at your partner since the goal of the activity is to simply practice being quiet and calm while being with another person.
4. As a group, answer the following question: "*How did it feel to be quiet and calm?*"

Activity #4: The Wonder of Listening

1. Change partners if there are more than two people.
2. As a group, discuss how to listen non-verbally (without talking) to another person. Possible discussion responses:
   - Sit quietly with ears open and mouth closed.
   - Lean toward the person.
   - Look at the person, showing interest in what he or she is saying.
   - Seek to understand what he or she is trying to say.
   - Do not react unnecessarily to the words the person is saying, but try to understand the feelings behind the words.
   - You may nod your head to show that you are listening to (not necessarily agreeing with) what is being said.
   - You may softly utter "*Uh-huh*" to the speaker.
3. Facing your partner, decide who will be Person A and who will be Person B.
4. A tells B about a favorite place to eat. B non-verbally listens to A (60 seconds or less), remembering not to talk!
5. Repeat the same activity but reverse the roles.
6. As a group, answer the following question: "*What did you feel and think when you were listened to by your partner?*"
7. As a group, answer the following question: "*What did you feel and think when you listened to your partner?*"

Activity #5: The Importance of Asking Clarifying Questions

1. Change partners if there are more than two people.

2. As a group, discuss why it is important to ask the speaker clarifying questions. Possible discussion responses:
   - Asking clarifying questions helps to keep the focus on the speaker.
   - When we ask clarifying questions, we ask questions that help the speaker explain more fully what he or she means.
   - When we ask clarifying questions, we seek to understand more clearly what the speaker is saying.
   - When we ask clarifying questions, we help the speaker think more deeply about the topic.

3. Examples of clarifying questions:
   "Can you tell me more about _____?"
   "Are you saying that _____?"
   "What did you mean by _____?"
   "What are you going to do?"
   "What if _____?"
   "Give me an example when you _____."
   "How did you feel when _____?"
   "Did this make you feel _____ (good; sad; angry; scared; happy; confused; joyous; unhappy; loved)?"
   "Where?" "When?" "Which?" "Why?"

4. Facing your partner, decide who will be Person A and who will be Person B.

5. A tells B about a favorite place to be alone. B non-verbally listens except to ask clarifying questions of A (two minutes or less).

6. Repeat the same activity but reverse the roles.

7. As a group, answer the following question: *"What did you feel and think when your partner listened to you and asked you clarifying questions?"*

8. As a group, answer the following question: *"What did you feel and think when you listened to your partner and asked clarifying questions?"*

Activity #6: The Power of Sending Direct Messages

1. Change partners if there are more than two people.
2. As a group, discuss ways to send direct messages to another person without taking away from or putting down the other person. There are three types of direct messages: a *feeling message,* an *encouraging message* and a *wonder message.*
3. Send a *feeling message*:
   - Consider what you, as a listener, are feeling and why.
   - Simply and sincerely state to the speaker what you are feeling and tell why.
   - Remember that you will have one or more feelings for any meaningful situation.
   - Examples of feeling words:

comfortable	uncomfortable	confused
happy	sad	glad
unhappy	frustrated	fearful
angry	tired	delighted
worried	exhausted	devastated
concerned	lonely	stupid
wild	confident	scared
joyous	nervous	hungry
love	negative	positive
insecure	terrible	terrific
excited	defeated	unsure
energetic	satisfied	horrible

   - Examples of feeling messages:
     "*I feel* _____ *because* _____."
     "*I feel* sad *because* I want us to be able to trust each other."
     "*I feel* angry and unhappy about what just happened *because* it seemed to be unkind."
     "*I feel* love *because* I received those beautiful flowers from you."
     "*I feel* concerned *because* you don't seem to understand how

much this situation affected me."

"*I feel* delighted *because* I believe you have given your best effort."

"*I feel* confused with what is happening *because* it doesn't seem to follow the plan we discussed."

"*I feel* sad *because* we have to cancel our vacation this year due to our current financial situation."

"*I feel* happy *because* we care about each other and *because* of our willingness to try to solve problems together."

4. Send an *encouraging message*:

- Encouragement inspires someone to give their best effort.
- Encouragement inspires someone to have courage and self-confidence.
- Examples of encouraging messages:

   "*I think you can do it! Give it a try!*"

   "*It's the little things that count.*"

   "*Give it your best effort.*"

   "*I will always be here for you.*"

   "*I don't think you'll know unless you try.*"

   "*Mistakes simply mean you have tried.*"

   "*I believe in you!*"

   "*I encourage you not to give up!*"

   "*I appreciate your courage.*"

5. Send a *wonder message*:

- A wonder message is used to address an uncomfortable issue.
- A wonder message is actually a question.
- A wonder message is used to express a thought.
- Examples of wonder messages:

   "*I wonder* _____?"

   "*I wonder* what you meant when you said _____?"

   "*I wonder* why we never talk?"

   "*I wonder* if you have forgiven me?"

   "*I wonder* if we really care enough about each other to risk going to see a family therapist?"

6. Facing your partner, decide who will be Person A and who will be Person B.

7. A tells B about a favorite vacation place. B non-verbally listens except to send direct messages (*feeling messages; encouraging messages; wonder messages*) to A (two minutes or less).

8. Repeat the same activity but reverse the roles.

9. As a group, answer the following question: "*What did you feel and think when your partner gave you direct messages?*"

10. As a group, answer the following question: "*What did you feel and think when you gave direct messages to your partner?*"

Activity #7: The Gift of Validating Statements

1. Change partners if there are more than two people.
2. As a group, discuss the following definitions and examples of validating statements:
   - A validating statement is a positive heart-felt message stated honestly and given freely to another person.
   - A validating statement is stated for no other reason than to let another person know how important he or she is to you.
3. Examples of validating statements:
   "I love you."
   "Thank you for being my _____ (son; daughter; wife; husband; mother; father; friend)*."*
   "I think we can get through anything together."
   "I am proud of the way you are trying in school."
   "I appreciate your willingness to keep working during these difficult times."
   "To me, you are a ray of sunshine."
   "Thanks for being you."
4. Facing your partner, decide who will be Person A and who will be Person B.
5. A tells B three to five things that are special about B or about someone A loves. B non-verbally listens to A (60 seconds or less).
6. Repeat the same activity but reverse the roles.
7. As a group, answer the following question: *"What did you think and feel when you heard validations?"*
8. As a group, answer the following question: *"What did you think and feel when you said validations?"*

Activity #8: The Significance of Self-affirming Statements

1. Change partners if there are more than two people.
2. As a group, discuss what it means to be self-affirming:
   - A self-affirming statement is a clear and positive message which you state honestly to yourself.
   - A self-affirming statement is always stated as if it is absolutely true.
   - A self-affirming statement is stated for no other reason than to reinforce how important you are as a human being.
   - Usually you say self-affirming statements quietly to yourself.
   - Positive messages said to you by others (validating statements) can become your own self-affirming statements.
   - Initially, you can practice self-affirming statements by acknowledging the *ValueSkills* you live each day.
3. Examples of self-affirming statements:
   "I am calm and gentle."
   "I am friendly."
   "I am encouraging."
   "I am considerate."
   "I am a good person."
   "I did a good job."
   "I am courteous."
   "I am respectful of property."
   "I am self-confident."
   "I am courageous."
   "I am a good leader."
   "I am a helpful person."
   "I am a caring person."
   "I am a sharing person."
   "I am enthusiastic."
   "I am respectful of others."

"*I am responsible.*"

"*I am humorous.*"

"*I am curious.*"

"*I am honest with kindness.*"

"*I am loving to my* _____ (son; daughter; father; mother; wife; husband)."

"*I remind myself of a* _____ (beautiful wild flower; playful kitten; protective shade tree)."

"*I am proud of the way I am trying in school.*"

"*I appreciate my willingness to keep working during difficult times.*"

4. Facing your partner, decide who will be Person A and who will be Person B.

5. A tells B three to five things that are special about himself or herself (30 seconds).

6. Repeat the same activity but reverse the roles.

7. As a group, answer the following question: "*What did you feel and think when you said self-affirming statements about yourself while another person listened?*"

8. As a group, answer the following question: "*What did you feel and think when you listened to your partner say self-affirming statements about him/herself?*"

Activity #9: The Delicate Nature of Direct Command Statements

1. This activity involves *adults only.*
2. This activity involves a discussion about using direct command statements with children.
3. Discuss definitions of direct command statements with the group:
   - Direct command statements are clear and direct messages that are stated honestly and firmly.
   - Direct command statements let another person know that you are concerned (safety issues) or upset (behavior issues) and expect immediate and cooperative action.
   - Direct command statements are used sparingly so they have an impact.
4. Examples of direct command statements for pre-school and primary-age children:

   "*I will give you until I count to three to stop what you are doing: one* (pause), *two* (pause)." If you reach number three, require the child to sit on a chair near you (time-out) for a specific number of minutes.

   "*Don't touch that stove!*"

   "*Please stop* _____ (a possible first warning)."

   "*I feel very frustrated! I want this stopped immediately* (a possible second warning)!"

   "*I want you to sit on the chair* (time-out on a chair near you) *for a few minutes and think about your behavior. Although I love you, your behavior is unacceptable* (a possible third warning for a violation of an important family rule or a continual problem)."

5. Examples of direct command statements for young children, intermediate-age children and young adults:

   "*I mean what I say.*"

   "*I expect you to do this immediately.*"

   "*I will not tolerate that tone of voice.*"

"I will not tolerate that kind of language."

"You may not go anywhere until we talk about your behavior."

6. Examples of direct command statements for intermediate-age children and young adults:

    "I feel frustrated! Please stop doing that immediately!"

    "I expect you to think about this issue and return with a solution that we can discuss."

    "Until we resolve this problem, you cannot _____

    (use the car; collect your allowance; leave for the party)."

    "We will discuss this later when both of us are feeling calm. In the meantime, I want you to think about what just happened."

    "Your behavior is inappropriate and unacceptable."

7. Direct command statements are effective when used sparingly. A rule to follow when disciplining children and young adults is to be firm, fair and loving. Children and young adults expect and need to have parents provide guidance, discipline and clear behavioral boundaries. Our hope is to discipline with resolve, with calmness and with dignity. If your child does not respond to your direct command statements, you may want to refer to the discipline approach, *Discipline with Calmness and Dignity*, found in Chapter Seven.

At first, looking for opportunities to model and reinforce these nine communication skills with our children may seem unnatural. *This is true when we try anything new.* To incorporate these skills into our lives, we need to consciously practice using them. Soon they will seem natural to us. As we use them, we foster greater understanding between family members and strengthen family relationships.

We can touch the hearts of our family members through more positive interactions. We can record positive images of ourselves in the hearts of those we love.

Disciplining children

can become

a major source of tension

not only between parents

and children,

but also between parents.

Chapter Six

Reward, Praise And Punishment Versus Discipline with Calmness And Dignity

For one moment, think of a family as being inside a circle. A family circle—really a ball if you visualize a three-dimensional structure—implies a confined area that holds values, rules and expectations. By visualizing different size spheres, we can graphically picture the differences in families, both in terms of the number of family members and their individual values, rules and expectations.

Family membership may include two-parent homes, joint and sole custody parenting households, blended families and foster care families. Over the years, family structures have become diverse and complex. Yet, regardless of the family configuration, disciplining children can become a major source of tension not only between parents and children, but also between parents. It is extremely difficult to be *fair* and *clear* and *firm* and *consistent* all at the same time.

The discipline approach presented in the next chapter, *Discipline with Calmness and Dignity,* reduces family tensions and provides a sense of order.

For a better understanding of the uniqueness and potential of this discipline approach, we begin by defining discipline, calmness and dignity:

Discipline:
- *informs* children of appropriate and expected behaviors, through teaching and modeling,
- *identifies* unacceptable behaviors that do not follow parental expectations,
- *re-directs* children's misbehaviors toward acceptable behaviors through dialogue and teaching,
- *solves* family problems and family issues,
- *establishes* positive individual and family goals,
- *provides* and *carries out* "appropriate and reasonable consequences" for misbehaviors, when necessary, and
- *seeks* outside-of-the-home support, when necessary.

Calmness is a state of mind. It does not imply acting in a cold or aloof manner. Rather, it allows us to acknowledge and express our thoughts and feelings appropriately and reasonably. Calmness means being in charge of our emotions, being in control of our voice and maintaining our composure. Since all parents need to deal with discipline, why not do it with the best chance of success? A key to this success is calmness.

Dignity generates respect for children. It recognizes a child's worth even during moments of conflict. Rather than criticizing a child, disciplining with dignity focuses on a specific behavior. Saying, "*I am unhappy that you did not put your toys away this morning. I want you to pick them up,*" is different than saying, "*You're lazy and a bad boy! Pick-up your toys immediately.*"

Discipline with Calmness and Dignity develops the traits, values and attitudes that produce individuals of good character. It is a process of positive steps parents take to teach and re-teach expected behaviors. It seeks to solve behavior problems rather than to simply punish a child for misbehaviors. It seeks to build upon mutual respect between parents and children.

Discipline with Calmness and Dignity is a departure from the practices of rewarding, praising and punishing which permeate most of our social institutions, particularly homes and schools. The following lists of characteristics help us compare these two approaches:

Reward, Praise and Punishment	Discipline with Calmness and Dignity
• provides external motivation (the motivation comes from others)	• provides internal motivation (the motivation comes from within the person)
• is based on power	• is based on mutual respect
• attempts to control	• attempts to guide
• develops reliance and resentment	• develops character and builds relationships

Punishment is usually a spur-of-the-moment response to correct "bad" behavior. Correcting children's misbehavior by using punishment, based on control, is often expressed by angry and insensitive responses. This usually brings about feelings of resentment in children.

Reward and praise are techniques that judge behavior as "good." They represent acknowledgment for doing what is expected by others. One reason for giving reward and praise is to motivate children to perform and achieve. Although reward and praise may seem appropriate on the surface, they tend to encourage a child's reliance on external compensations. Over time, the child learns to cooperate only to gain such external rewards or to avoid punishment. On a more subtle level, children learn to rely on other's judgments in formulating their sense of worth and sense of competence.

In contrast, *Discipline with Calmness and Dignity* fosters mutual respect between parents and children. This discipline approach teaches *ValueSkills* (basic common values), helps children develop respect and responsibility and lets them know what is expected. It re-directs misbehavior into acceptable behavior through dialogue and teaching. Together, parents and children resolve family issues through problem-solving techniques. When necessary, parents initiate reasonable and appropriate consequences for a child's misbehavior.

The following three figures depict the differences between reward, praise and punishment and *Discipline with Calmness and Dignity.*

*Reward and praise are external
motivation techniques.*

giving to a child
for being the best

basing a child's value
on production

basing a child's
value on
competition

REWARD
and PRAISE
INVOLVE

giving to a child
for winning

giving as a form
of motivation

basing a
child's worth
on other
people's
opinions

motivating a
child only if
the reward and
praise continue

motivating through
external means

Punishment is an external motivation technique.

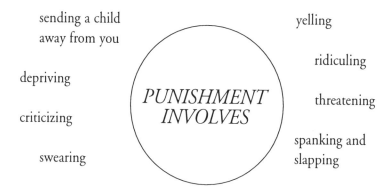

sending a child
away from you

depriving

criticizing

swearing

PUNISHMENT
INVOLVES

yelling

ridiculing

threatening

spanking and
slapping

Discipline with Calmness and Dignity is an internal motivation approach.

using 'time-out'
(a place near you)
for reflection

loving your
child
unconditionally

using fair and
appropriate
consequences

DISCIPLINE INVOLVES

staying calm
and focused
with your child

discussing
which *ValueSkills*
your child has
violated

letting your
child know
how you feel

working to solve
problems together

listening to
and talking
with your child

Reward, praise and punishment are all forms of external motivation that interrelate. All three techniques are used widely by parents, teachers, bosses, coaches and, of course, kids. These behavioral approaches are what most of us learned as children.

Most of us can remember the pleasure of receiving rewards and praise—whether it came from our parents or from others. We can also remember the disappointment of not receiving praise when we expected it, or the fear and uncertainty we felt anticipating punishment.

As we grew and matured, we began to rely on such external motivations, basing our behaviors on other people's demands and expectations; this is particularly true with regard to rules, academic success and athletic victory. It didn't take long until these external motivation techniques became our way of doing business.

Things have not changed much in 40 years. My grandson was upset the night before he started first grade because he was afraid he would not get all A's in school. A neighbor told him that he was so smart, he was sure to get all A's. Already, this child was facing the anxieties associated with external expectations. In school, students experience praise, threats, A's, F's and even visits to the principal's office as sources of external power. But the *power game* between teachers and students does not build relationships, mutual respect and healthy character traits in students. And for a large number of students, it does not result in order, completed homework and good grades.

Such *power games* also occur in our homes:
Conflicts arise,
parent-child battles ensue,
children resist,
parents resort to control and punishment techniques
battles escalate
children feel resentment, and
parents feel defeated.

72

Often, the result is a stand-off between parents and children.

We use reward, praise and punishment because it is what we know. In the short-term, the approach seems to work. Certainly, to a degree, reward, praise and punishment are going to continue to be an inextricable part of our parenting practices. But I suggest that we make *Discipline with Calmness and Dignity* our primary approach.

We must talk to our children

with calmness and

treat them with dignity to

enhance their self-confidence and

self-worth and strengthen

their sense of security.

Chapter Seven

Discipline With Calmness And Dignity

D*iscipline with Calmness and Dignity* does not set up a struggle for power between parents and children, as does the system of re-ward, praise and punishment. The goal of this unique approach is to develop a home climate where parents and children have respect for one another.

Before we discuss the stages of this discipline approach, consider a few suggestions for dealing with your child during difficult moments:

- Take time to gain perspective when you are facing a problem you don't know how to handle. Consider what actions will create a more nurturing and positive relationship before dealing with your child.

- If what you are doing isn't working, think about what changes you can make. Sometimes doing things differently brings about a new awareness for all parties involved.

- Deal with an issue when you aren't already stressed by other things.

- When you are involved in a situation that begins to escalate, recognize that it is time to stop what is going on and continue when things have calmed down.

- Focus on what your child does right rather than simply concentrating on what your child does wrong.

Discipline with Calmness and Dignity is a four-stage approach that includes teaching, talking, problem-solving and seeking additional support when needed. A different statement highlights each of the four stages of discipline:

- Stage One: Teaching—"*This is what we expect from each other.*"
- Stage Two: Talking—"*We need to talk.*"
- Stage Three: Problem-Solving—"*This is a serious matter.*"
- Stage Four: Seeking Additional Support—"*Our family needs help.*"

The following pages provide more in-depth information regarding the four stages of discipline.

Stage One - Teaching

The first stage of discipline is a prevention stage to be used when there is no discipline problem occuring. It introduces the 14 *Value-Skills* necessary for bringing harmony to our homes. As I think of my own family, I know the pleasure and delight I feel when all of our behaviors exemplify these common inner strengths.

ValueSkills include:

ValueSkills I	*ValueSkills II*
1. being a good listener	8. being considerate
2. being friendly	9. being courteous
3. being kind	10. being respectful of property
4. being cooperative	11. being responsible for personal care
5. being encouraging	
6. being honest (with kindness)	12. being self-confident
7. being patient	13. being enthusiastic
	14. being courageous

Stage One involves modeling the 14 *ValueSkills* in our own behaviors. It involves teaching the benefits and significance of them to our children. Family activities in Chapters Nine and Ten are created specifically for teaching the 14 *ValueSkills* to children. *ValueSkills* can also be reinforced by observing and discussing situations in everyday life. These real life situations provide opportunities to talk about whether people are using or not using *ValueSkills*. Experiencing the activities and talking together builds a base for understanding what family members need and expect from one another.

As we teach our children, it is important to include the "Principle of Reciprocity"—*What you need from me, I need from you* and the "Golden Rule"—*Treat others the way you want to be treated.* As we interact with our children, we also need to practice the parenting, communication and team-building skills presented in earlier chapters and remember to teach and practice calmness.

Summary
    Stage One: Teaching—*"This is what we expect from each other."*
• *Teach* and *Model* calmness and the 14 *ValueSkills*
• *Teach* and *Model* the "Golden Rule"
• *Practice* the parenting, communication and team-building skills presented in earlier chapters

Stage Two - Talking

This stage involves the parent and child discussing the child's misbehavior. In their discussion, they explore why it happened, identifying more appropriate ways to handle the situation and reviewing the *ValueSkill(s)* that relates to the unacceptable behavior.

Every misbehavior relates to at least one of the 14 ValueSkills.

The *ValueSkill(s)* becomes the focus of the discussion with the child. It may be helpful for parents to refer to the information about a particular *ValueSkill* in Chapter Nine or Ten. There is no need to over-react. It is important to use effective parenting and communication skills while supporting and guiding the child toward more appropriate behaviors.

As parents, we need to stay calm, listen to our children and talk about our relationships with each other. Stage Two challenges us to replace over-reacting and yelling with listening and talking; to substitute blaming and denying with caring and sharing; to forgo bribing and punishing in favor of discussing and correcting. This stage simply and appropriately says, "*We need to talk.*"

It is not always necessary, however, to talk with our children about every error in judgment. Parents are continually in a position to make decisions about when to respond to and when to ignore attention-getting and controlling behaviors. For this reason we need to choose wisely the issues we pursue with our children. It is sometimes appropriate and reasonable to ignore undesirable behaviors. These might include:

- a slip of the tongue by a child that is crude but not vulgar,
- an argument between a child and a friend or between two siblings that is annoying but not destructive or harmful,
- a statement by a child that stretches the truth, and
- an unkind word or unfriendly gesture that is presented as a result of an emotional situation, but is not significantly unacceptable.

In this stage, we serve as teachers, caretakers, advisers, cheerleaders, taskmasters, counselors and team-builders. We are the people in charge. We create the home climate and set the stage for talking things over. We are the leaders who keep things in order, perspective and harmony. In these varied roles, we must be able to communicate effectively with our children. We also need to consider the circumstances of difficult situations before making decisions about how to deal with them.

For example, imagine a scenario in which a child refuses to eat lunch before leaving on a trip. The family is going to be driving for four hours before stopping for dinner. The parent should consider the possible reasons for the child's behavior. The child's responses (verbal and non-verbal) determine the parent's response. The child's age is also a factor. The goal is to understand and communicate effectively with the child.

As we teach and discuss *ValueSkills* through the first two stages of discipline, we find ourselves treating our children with more respect. In turn, our children act friendlier and more cooperative.

Summary

Stage Two: Talking—"*We need to talk.*"

- *Discuss* the misbehavior and *Talk* about the specific *ValueSkill(s)* which is not being practiced
- *Re-Teach* and *Model* the *ValueSkill(s)* which is not being practiced
- *Practice* the parenting, communication and team-building skills presented in earlier chapters

Stage Three - Problem-solving

We all experience disappointments and make mistakes, even though we try our best and encourage our children to do the same. Throughout life, we continue to encounter problems: some may be small, requiring relatively little effort, and others may be large, demanding a great deal of time and energy. As some of us painfully know, there are also problems that do not go away, but continue to be part of life. It is vital to learn how to deal with problems within our families.

Deciding when to move into the problem-solving stage is a personal choice. Each of us must decide when to say, "*This is a serious matter."* My dad often said, *"Whether you have within you a large sponge* (a high degree of tolerance) *or a small sponge* (a low degree of tolerance), *when your sponge is full, it's full."* When you feel like you are "walking on eggs" or losing a sense of order and harmony in your home, it is time to take appropriate and reasonable action.

I believe that the best action to take at this time includes family problem-solving. Those involved could include any combination of family members, the entire family or extended family members. Family problem-solving is an effective process for defining the problem, generating possible solutions, selecting one solution to try and evaluating the results.

A Problem-solving Approach
Step One: Describe the problem

Family members listen carefully to the person who has a concern. This person provides as many details as possible so that everyone involved can more fully understand the nature of the concern.

Step Two: Ask questions to clarify the problem

Family members ask clarifying questions (see Chapter Five— Activity Five) about the problem being described to better understand the situation. When the problem-solvers (family members) understand the details of the problem, move on to Step Three.

Step Three: Identify three to five possible solutions

During this part of the problem-solving process, family members generate three to five possible solutions. The person who described the problem listens as other family members propose solutions. It is important that the person with the problem avoid saying things like *"It won't work,"* or *"I tried that before":* he or she should just listen, asking clarifying questions when necessary. Remaining calm and practicing good listening skills are essential facets of the experience, ensuring that a vital piece of a solution being presented is not lost. Be sure to write down the suggestions.

Step Four: Choose a solution

After all of the solutions are presented, the person with the concern chooses (a) one of the solutions, (b) a combination of two or more of the solutions, or (c) a completely different solution to solve the problem. After deciding which course of action to take, make a note of the decision.

Step Five: Report the results

After the solution has been tried, family members meet again to determine whether the issue has been resolved. At this time the person who introduced the concern evaluates the results.

• Did the solution solve the problem? Why/why not?
• What worked and what did not work?
• What did you learn from the experience?
• If the problem is not solved, do you want to try one of the other suggested solutions or do you want to think about other possible solutions by doing the family problem-solving activity again?

This five-step problem-solving strategy teaches children and parents the power of working together. It teaches family members that they need not struggle alone with a concern, that the family can be a significant support system. It teaches families to be inventive: that there are many ways to approach a problem and that it may take several attempts before it is resolved.

Allow for Appropriate and Reasonable Consequences

A significant part of problem-solving involves experiencing consequences. Children often learn best when consequences occur naturally. Letting children learn that there is a reaction for nearly everything they say and do teaches them the concept of "cause and effect." This in turn helps them anticipate possible consequences before acting.

As parents, we often want to protect our children from experiencing negative consequences. We want to rescue them from the effects of their own behaviors. But we need to let them experience the consequences of their actions, as long as they are not potentially harmful. Consequences often become more serious as our children grow into adulthood. At that point, we can no longer "save" them from what might happen. If we do not allow them to experience consequences when they are young, we are essentially preventing them from learning valuable lessons.

There are times when we need to determine consequences for our children's misbehaviors. These are times when natural consequences are unsafe or will occur so far in the future that children may not fully understand the long term implications of their behaviors. There are also times when the result of a behavior affects others negatively and therefore must be stopped. During such times parents need to take responsibility for setting boundaries, determining what behaviors will be tolerated, clearly stating what consequences will occur and following through, when necessary.

An appropriate consequence fits the "crime." For example, when six year-old Peter continues to yell and scream in the store, it is time to remove him from the scene. If his father chooses not to take him along to the store the next time he is going, Peter will probably learn a valuable lesson. He might be willing to demonstrate cooperation and courtesy when his father takes him along on a future visit to the store. Cooperation and courtesy are two important *ValueSkills* that Peter's father needs to discuss with Peter so that he understands why the privilege to go on the second trip to the store was taken away.

Reasonable consequences are fair in duration and severity. When nine-year old Molly is having a particularly bad day, complaining and arguing with her little sister, it is reasonable to tell her to sit for ten minutes and think about her behavior. After ten minutes, be prepared to discuss the situation and any *ValueSkills* that she didn't follow. It would be unreasonable to make her sit for 60 minutes.

In the same way, if twelve year old Edward is 30 minutes late for dinner because he forgot the time, a discussion will probably suffice. But if it is the third time this week he has been late for dinner, it seems appropriate and reasonable to have him play in his own yard the next day, missing the neighborhood football game. I would also encourage Edward's parents to re-teach and promote cooperation, consideration and being a good listener, three important *ValueSkills,* in order for him to assume responsibility for getting home on time.

Consequences are important learning tools. We need to use good judgment in deciding which natural consequences are safe for our children and which ones put them at risk. We also need to determine carefully the consequences we set up to be sure they are appropriate and reasonable.

"I Mean What I Say"

There are times when your child will test you to a point of exhaustion. Consider the following thoughts when you are feeling challenged and frustrated by your child:

- Stay calm and try to listen to both the feelings and the thoughts of the child. Take enough time to consider a reasonable and appropriate response.
- Remember that your home is "your castle." Take the lead by being responsible for creating the climate in your home.
- Draw an authority line between yourself and your child. This is the line that declares, "*I am the parent and you are the child.*"

Listed below are a few parent responses you can use when you need to assert your leadership with children and young adults (see Chapter Five—Direct Command Statements):

"*I mean what I say.*"

"*I will not tolerate that tone of voice.*"

"*We will discuss this later when both of us are feeling calm. In the meantime, I want you to think about what just happened.*"

"*Your behavior is inappropriate and unacceptable.*"

As you assess your situation, ask the following questions:

- Have you reviewed the discipline stages identified in this chapter?

- Are you using the parenting, communication and team-building skills, as well as *ValueSkills* described in this book?

- Have you spent time with your family understanding the problem and discussing possible ways to solve it?

- Does each family member, or the family as a whole, have one or more goals aimed at enhancing family relationships and family unity?

- Do you sense a commitment from everyone in your family to try to improve relationships or do you sense an effort to sabotage and erode family unity?

Many families experience times when everything seems to be going wrong, frustrations are high and problems seem insurmountable. These are times when someone objective and neutral may be needed to help get the family back on track. You may need to move on to Stage Four.

Summary

Stage Three: Problem-Solving— *"This is a serious matter."*

- *Call* a meeting of an appropriate combination of family members, the entire family or extended family members to identify and solve problems

- *Clarify* and *Discuss* the problem

- *Brainstorm* possible solutions to solve the problem
- *Choose* and *Implement* one solution
- *Call* a follow-up meeting with the family members involved to evaluate the results of implementing the problem-solving solution
- *Set* boundaries and *Allow* for appropriate and reasonable consequences, when necessary
- Be willing to *Say,* "*I am the parent and you are the child*", when necessary

Stage Four - Seeking Additional Support

As parents, we need to determine at what point outside help is needed for our families. My advice to parents is to seek help when nothing seems to be working, when family members are confused and burdened by their feelings and perceptions and when it seems that the family is falling apart and basic family values are disintegrating.

Getting help is within our reach and power. It can be as basic as visiting a friend or relative for advice or as comprehensive as consulting a team of child developmental specialists. Examine the family needs and consider the options available. A meeting with school personnel, a visit with a pediatrician, a heart-to-heart talk with a religious leader, joining a support group or visits with a professional therapist (individual; marriage; family) are all options that can help a family put things in perspective.

The more quickly we reach out for help when our families are not in harmony, the easier it is to resolve conflicts and return to the behaviors and attitudes that we want in our homes.

Summary
Stage Four: Seeking Additional Support—"*Our family needs help.*"
- *Option:* Parent(s) participates in a parent support group or parenting seminar

- *Option:* Appropriate family members meet with a respected person (relative; friend; religious leader)
- *Option:* Parent(s) meets with the child's teacher(s) and, when appropriate, the child
- *Option:* Parent(s) and child meet with a pediatrician for a physical examination and a review of the child's medical history
- *Option:* Appropriate family members meet with a professional mental health worker (individual; marriage; family)
- *Option:* Parent(s) and child meet with a child developmental team for a complete evaluation

Remember that a discouraged child, a lonely child, a child with poor ("*No one likes me*") self-esteem and a child with negative ("*I don't like myself*") self-esteem may seek attention and control through misbehavior.

There are other reasons why a child misbehaves, including anxiety, fear, failure, problems with paying attention and concentrating, environmental illness (symptoms caused by environmental circumstances), traumatic childhood experiences, personal concerns, medical problems, addictions and chemical dependency. The more time we spend in meaningful and caring dialogue with our children, the less we will have to worry about dealing with attention-getting and controlling behaviors from them.

Disciplining with Calmness and Dignity fosters mutual respect and harmony within our families.

Every day we prove to the world those things that we believe about ourselves. It is for this reason that we must talk to our children with calmness and treat them with dignity in order to enhance their self-confidence and self-worth, and strengthen their sense of security.

*A child who feels discouraged
needs encouragement
—not more disapproval.*

*A child who feels lonely
needs friendship
—not more isolation.*

*A child who feels disliked
needs acceptance
—not more rejection.*

*A child who feels unworthy,
needs appreciation
—not more criticism.*

We can bring about

the necessary changes

that will enrich our lives

and the lives

of those we love.

Chapter Eight

As A Parent, I Will Remember…

As a parent, I will remember to listen more, really listen to my children and focus on the feelings behind their words and behind their anger. I will encourage more, ask more questions and express more feelings. I will stay calm and over-react less often. I will make each day count.

As a parent, I will post the ValueSkills where I can see them each day. I will teach them, promote them, model them and, when necessary, demand them. I will understand when my children fall short of these ideals and admit my own shortcomings. I will say "I forgive you" and "I'm sorry" more often. I will let go of the things that I cannot change. I will take more time to talk with my family about the joys and frustrations and the successes and struggles in each of our lives. I will more openly model my values, share my religious beliefs and discuss my political views. I will remember to spend more time alone with each member of my family and seek their help in solving problems and setting up goals.

As a parent, I will love each member of my family unconditionally. I will love my children enough to set boundaries and maintain fair and wholesome standards in my home. And I will love them enough to know where they go and what they do. I will allow them to learn the vital lessons of safe, natural consequences. I will tell my children when their actions are inappropriate and I will remember that sometimes they need firm, tough guidance and sometimes they need tender, affectionate support. I will express my feelings and thoughts in clear, simple language.

As a parent, I will encourage my children to have the courage to resist the temptations and social pressures for smoking, drinking alcohol, using illegal drugs and gambling. I will closely monitor what my children watch on television and the music they hear. I will teach and model good nutrition, exercise and relaxation.

I will read more with my children. I will help them gain self-confidence and encourage them to treat others with dignity and practice "The Golden Rule." I will establish family traditions, enjoy family adventures together and laugh more often with my family.

As a parent, I will teach my children how to prioritize their activities, organize their school work and budget their money. I will expect them to do chores, clean up after themselves and take pride in their home.

As a parent, I will remember to be positive, open and loving. I will be firm, fair and consistent. I will celebrate little things with enthusiasm and sing more often with my family. I will remember to say special things to members of my family, such as "Thank you," "Please," "Let me help you," "Thanks for being you," "Go ahead and try," "I'm proud of you" and "I love you as you are."

As a parent, I will remember to travel a path that says, "I will walk with you, support you, guide you, teach you and love you until the end of time."

Through our actions, we can be positive influences—not only as parents, but as grandparents, aunts, uncles, teachers, friends, colleagues and leaders. Regardless of the roles we play, we can make significant contributions by demonstrating positive attitudes and behaviors as we interact with others.

None of us can be perfect parents. We can only strive to do our best. Some of us are just beginning the lifelong journey of parenting. Others are further along the parenting path. Either way, we can become better prepared to anticipate and deal with the hidden potholes we encounter.

By examining how we respond to our children, we can begin to make necessary changes toward more positive and effective interactions. Developing closer relationships with our children helps us be prepared for recognizing danger signs in their behaviors. It helps us set clear boundaries for them.

Together, we can bring about the necessary changes that will enrich our lives and the lives of those we love. We want the very best for our children. It is possible to have a parenting philosophy that better prepares our children for tomorrow's world. We need to find time to look into the hearts of our children.

After reading the information in this book, you can examine your approach to parenting by thinking about and defining how you choose to act, what you want to teach your child and the types of relationships you want to develop in your family. Gradually, you will be able to put these thoughts into practice.

The following *Parenting Checklist* will help you examine your current parenting style, highlight the positive ways you nurture your child and help you recognize areas needing improvement.

Parenting Checklist

Read the following questions. Circle the number that best describes your position, ranging from "1" meaning you don't use the particular skill to "9" meaning you consistently use it. Generally, a "1," "2" or "3" means you are not using this skill at all or have barely begun to practice it; a "4," "5" or "6" means you have started to incorporate this skill into your daily behavior but it has not yet become a consistent part of your parenting approach; and a "7," "8" or "9" means you are successfully and regularly using this skill.

1. Am I meeting these parenting challenges effectively? (see Chapter One)
   - loving my child unconditionally   1 2 3 4 5 6 7 8 9
   - expressing feelings constructively 1 2 3 4 5 6 7 8 9
   - living in the present   1 2 3 4 5 6 7 8 9
   - setting boundaries   1 2 3 4 5 6 7 8 9
   - making character development
     a priority   1 2 3 4 5 6 7 8 9

2. Am I using the parenting skills effectively? (see Chapter Three)
   - staying calm   1 2 3 4 5 6 7 8 9
   - listening to my child   1 2 3 4 5 6 7 8 9
   - encouraging my child   1 2 3 4 5 6 7 8 9
   - using *ValueSkills* in my daily life 1 2 3 4 5 6 7 8 9
   - giving my child appropriate attention 1 2 3 4 5 6 7 8 9
   - giving my child appropriate responses 1 2 3 4 5 6 7 8 9
   - explaining my feelings and thoughts
     briefly and clearly   1 2 3 4 5 6 7 8 9
   - allowing for compromise   1 2 3 4 5 6 7 8 9
   - allowing for consequences   1 2 3 4 5 6 7 8 9
   - apologizing when appropriate   1 2 3 4 5 6 7 8 9

3. Am I using the team-building skills effectively? (see Chapter Four)
   - having my family do the *ValueSkills*
     activities in Chapters Nine and Ten 1 2 3 4 5 6 7 8 9
   - living the *ValueSkills* so my child
     sees them in my actions   1 2 3 4 5 6 7 8 9
   - applauding family members for
     good effort   1 2 3 4 5 6 7 8 9

- working with my family on
  goal setting   1 2 3 4 5 6 7 8 9

4. Am I using the communication
   skills effectively? (see Chapter Five)
   - not ignoring others   1 2 3 4 5 6 7 8 9
   - not interrupting others   1 2 3 4 5 6 7 8 9
   - being calm so I can express
     myself clearly   1 2 3 4 5 6 7 8 9
   - listening in order to understand   1 2 3 4 5 6 7 8 9
   - asking clarifying questions   1 2 3 4 5 6 7 8 9
   - sending direct messages to let others
     know how I feel and what I think   1 2 3 4 5 6 7 8 9
   - appreciating others by saying
     validating statements   1 2 3 4 5 6 7 8 9
   - giving myself affirmations of my
     special qualities   1 2 3 4 5 6 7 8 9
   - using direct command statements
     when necessary   1 2 3 4 5 6 7 8 9

5. Am I doing the following as I
   discipline my child *with Calmness
   and Dignity?* (see Chapter Six)
   - taking charge as a parent   1 2 3 4 5 6 7 8 9
   - setting appropriate boundaries
     for my child   1 2 3 4 5 6 7 8 9
   - providing love and firmness   1 2 3 4 5 6 7 8 9

6. Am I using the *Discipline with
   Calmness and Dignity* stages
   effectively? (see Chapter Seven)

- teaching and modeling the
  14 *ValueSkills*   1 2 3 4 5 6 7 8 9
- discussing with my child why a
  misbehavior happened   1 2 3 4 5 6 7 8 9
- exploring more appropriate ways to
  handle the situation and re-teaching
  the *ValueSkill(s)* that is not
  being used   1 2 3 4 5 6 7 8 9
- problem-solving by defining a
  problem, discussing solutions,
  trying a solution and evaluating
  the outcome   1 2 3 4 5 6 7 8 9
- seeking outside help for my family
  when necessary   1 2 3 4 5 6 7 8 9

7. Am I demonstrating the following
   parenting behaviors?
   (see Chapter Eight)
   - providing security for my child   1 2 3 4 5 6 7 8 9
   - having fun and sharing adventures
     with my child   1 2 3 4 5 6 7 8 9
   - spending quality time with my child 1 2 3 4 5 6 7 8 9
   - showing respect for myself and for
     family members   1 2 3 4 5 6 7 8 9
   - assuming responsibility for my actions 1 2 3 4 5 6 7 8 9
   - treating others with dignity   1 2 3 4 5 6 7 8 9
   - acting with integrity in my
     interactions with others   1 2 3 4 5 6 7 8 9

8. Am I teaching my child *ValueSkills I*
   as well as modeling them?
   (see Chapter Nine)

- being a good listener   1 2 3 4 5 6 7 8 9
- being friendly   1 2 3 4 5 6 7 8 9
- being kind   1 2 3 4 5 6 7 8 9
- being cooperative   1 2 3 4 5 6 7 8 9
- being encouraging   1 2 3 4 5 6 7 8 9
- being honest (with kindness)   1 2 3 4 5 6 7 8 9
- being patient   1 2 3 4 5 6 7 8 9

9. Am I teaching my child *ValueSkills II*
   as well as modeling them?
   (see Chapter Ten)
   - being considerate   1 2 3 4 5 6 7 8 9
   - being courteous   1 2 3 4 5 6 7 8 9
   - being respectful of property   1 2 3 4 5 6 7 8 9
   - being responsible for personal care   1 2 3 4 5 6 7 8 9
   - being self-confident   1 2 3 4 5 6 7 8 9
   - being enthusiastic   1 2 3 4 5 6 7 8 9
   - being courageous   1 2 3 4 5 6 7 8 9

After completing the Parenting Checklist take note of the areas you practice consistently, those you practice sometimes and those that need to be added to your parenting approach. Review the parenting checklist periodically to remind yourself of those things you want to do to be a more effective parent.

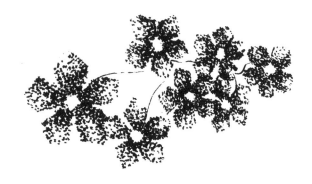

The seven ValueSkills I are:

being a good listener,

being friendly,

being kind,

being cooperative,

being encouraging,

being honest (with kindness)

and being patient.

Chapter Nine

Family Activities For Teaching ValueSkills® I

We are our children's first and most important teachers. Our children learn from us: tasks, responsibilities, attitudes, and, yes, values. We all have values that we want to pass along to our children. Seeing them act upon these inner strengths gives us a sense of pleasure, accomplishment and pride. Watching these behaviors develop expands our respect for our sons and daughters as they become young adults.

As science and technology continue to advance and our world becomes less personalized, we need, more than ever, to focus on building character and integrity. This happens as we teach and model the values we hold dear and foster the skills necessary to live those values each day. Essential common values that we can teach as skills are called *ValueSkills*.

The seven *ValueSkills I* in this chapter include:

listening

friendliness

kindness

cooperation

encouragement

honesty (with kindness)

patience

What sets *ValueSkills* apart from other values? They are the basic values from which other values evolve. They are the foundation for building strong character. For example, I find it difficult for many children to understand and act upon respect and responsibility as social values; without first having these terms reduced to more basic values, such as friendliness, kindness and cooperation. Only after children internalize the basic *ValueSkills* do they begin to understand the more complex concepts of respect and responsibility.

Spending time together exploring *ValueSkills* can become a rewarding family experience. Being teachers and role models for our children is a tremendous responsibility and a special opportunity, one to be cherished. It is an opportunity for developing respect, responsibility and a cohesive family.

While learning about *ValueSkills* we need to focus on:

• helping our children gain awareness of each *ValueSkill,* and

• encouraging them to put *ValueSkills* into practice.

There are a total of 14 *ValueSkills* sections in Chapters Nine and Ten that are learning guides for family times together. All the sections have been designed purposely to follow the same outline in a workbook fashion. This helps each family member become familiar with the format and anticipate what's next. The activities are easy to follow and require little or no preparation for parents.

When teaching a *ValueSkill,* it is important to follow the activities in order. The activities are designed so that family members can achieve maximum internalization of the *ValueSkill*. To review how the internalization process works, reexamine the information on internalizing values in Chapter Three.

Before teaching a *ValueSkill* to children, parents need to:

- preview the *"Definitions and Thoughts"* and *"Benefits"* sections of the *ValueSkill* to be explored,
- consider what should be discussed and understood about the *ValueSkill*,
- set a tone of calmness, and
- let each person know there are safeguards when participating in the activities. Explain that it is important for each family member to practice the safeguards to prevent hurt feelings and family squabbles.

Safeguards

1. Do not discuss things that might embarrass other family members.
2. What family members say must be respected and held in confidence (do not talk to others about family discussions).
3. Each family member has the right to "pass" (to say nothing if he or she so chooses).
4. *Treat others the way you want to be treated.*

As A Family:

- define each *ValueSkill* and talk about why it is important,
- use the activities provided, including *Mealtime Discussion Questions, Circle Time Topics, Quick and Easy Family Projects, Family Activities* and *Sentence Completions* to introduce and teach *ValueSkills*,
- encourage each other to practice *ValueSkills* and congratulate each other for putting *ValueSkills* into action,
- select books, music, movies and artistic performances to

share that provide opportunities for talking about each *ValueSkill,*

- post on the family message board the *ValueSkills* which are being discussed and practiced, and
- look for real life events or people that illustrate *ValueSkills* in action or being ignored.

The 14 *ValueSkills* sections don't need to be introduced in the order they are presented. If a situation prompts the introduction of a particular *ValueSkill* it is an opportune time for learning.

My hope is that families will have meaningful discussions, enjoyable times and tender moments while experiencing the activities. These family interactions will create long lasting bonds between family members.

Explore *ValueSkills* with enthusiasm and confidence. Practice patience and maintain a sense of humor. When first trying the activities, a family's time together may only last for a few minutes. If the experiences are enjoyed, the amount of time a family spends together will increase and gradually family interactions will become more meaningful. I recommend that families eventually participate in the activities for two 20 to 30-minute periods per week. This will provide continuity in experiences. The best chance for successful family interaction is to have scheduled meeting times so that everyone can plan to be available.

Not all of the thoughts and activities provided are appropriate for very young children. It may be necessary to wait to present some of them until children are older, although simple variations in format may make them appropriate for pre-school children. Many activities can be used over and over again as children grow.

Learning about the *ValueSkills* is most effective if both parents participate in teaching and modeling them. Doing the activities with extended family members or other families can further serve to reinforce the importance of what is being taught by letting children know that others also support these ideas and values. Having the involvement of others can be especially helpful if children are reluctant to participate. When people outside the immediate family are involved, children tend to be more cooperative and, in turn, learn and enjoy the time together.

If children refuse to take part in these family activities, it is a clear warning sign that problems exist. Remember a basic premise of this book: stay calm, be loving, be firm, be the parent-in-charge. As parents, we need to set the boundaries for expected behaviors. We also need to remember to follow the safeguards stated earlier in this chapter as we do the family activities together.

Doing the *ValueSkills* activities is like anything else we do for the first time: the more often we practice something, the more comfortable and proficient we become at it. As we continue to spend time experiencing the activities we will build stronger family bonds.

ValueSkills® I Family Activities are presented on the following pages.

Listening

*I'm reminded of a friend who one day overheard her
daughter singing along with great enthusiasm to an old
song on the radio. The song lyrics indicated that "there's a
bad moon on the rise." But this pint size rocker sang "there's
a bathroom on the right," and she couldn't be talked out
of her version. Sometimes what we think we hear and
what is being said are two very different things.*

Definitions and Thoughts

Listening is a combination of hearing, interpreting and thinking. It requires the listener to focus attention on what is being said
and then to think about what it means. The listener needs to pay
careful attention to the way something is said, as well as to the
speaker's body language. Every message is a combination of a feeling(s)
and a thought(s).

To listen effectively you need to be quiet when someone is
speaking. Look at the person who is talking and concentrate on
what is being said. You might nod your head or lean forward to let
the speaker know that you are paying attention. Ask questions if
you need further information or if there is something you don't
understand. Take notes if it is important to remember what is being said.

Listening:

- is watching another person's facial expressions,
- is being attentive to the words another person chooses,
- is hearing the feelings behind the words,
- is hearing what is being said,
- is being aware of body language, and
- is being alert to the sounds of nature.

Benefits

Listening:
- helps you understand what a person is trying to say,
- allows you to get to know someone better,
- shows that you care about the speaker's ideas, thoughts and feelings, and
- helps you gain new information and knowledge.

Mealtime Discussion Questions

Why is listening an important skill to have?

What are the qualities of a good listener?

Do you ever sit quietly and listen to the sounds around you?

Can you sometimes tell what a person is feeling just by watching his or her facial expressions and body movements?
Give examples.

Do you believe that most people are good listeners?
Why/why not?

Circle Time Topics

Focus On Personal Experiences

Have your family sit in a circle. When everyone is comfortable, a family member reads the first "circle time topic" below to the rest of the family. Each member takes a turn talking about a personal experience relating to the topic. Other family members ask clarifying questions (see Chapter Five). Your family can continue discussing the second and third "circle time topics" if time permits.

Discuss a time when:
- you were a good listener.
    a. Did you enjoy listening to this person?
    b. Did you feel that this person appreciated your listening skills?

- another person listened to you when you needed to talk to someone.
    a. How well do you know this person?
    b. Did you feel that this person understood what you were saying?
- someone told you something and you were glad you listened.
    a. How was the information useful?
    b. Did you ever tell the person that the information was helpful?

A Quick and Easy Family Project
A Flower Garden

As a family, draw a flower garden on a large sheet of paper that visually expresses calmness. Each family member explains why the flower garden makes him or her feel calm. Each person is asked to explain why he or she is a better listener when in a calm setting.

Family Activity #1
Relaxation

Listening is simply attending to others in a calm and non-judgmental way. Listed below are a few basic relaxation techniques which can help family members prepare for attending:

1. Deep breathing: Taking deep breaths is one of the best ways to relax. When you are feeling tense, angry or sad, take a few deep breaths. Relax your body and slowly fill your lungs with air, then slowly breathe out through your mouth.

2. Body relaxation: This is an activity you can use alone whenever you feel stressed or just want to relax. To practice this activity, one person reads the directions slowly as the other family members follow the directions.

    Close your eyes while breathing deeply and relax. Begin by focusing on your feet. Tighten your toes and then relax them

104

while thinking how marvelous it is to be able to walk and run.

Do a similar procedure for each of the other parts of your body: tighten and relax your right leg; tighten and relax your left leg; tighten and relax your torso; tighten and relax your right arm; tighten and relax your left arm; squeeze your right fist and relax; squeeze your left fist and relax; tighten and relax your neck and face. Continue to relax for several minutes.

3. Take an imaginary trip: Think about being in a place where you can totally relax. Close your eyes, take a few deep breaths and imagine you have gone to this place. See yourself as you walk on warm sand, swim in cool water, or hike in a quiet forest; feel the gentle breeze upon your face as you ride a horse, walk alone on an empty country road, sit on rocks above a misty sea or stand on top of a majestic mountain. Continue your imaginary trip for several minutes.

Family Activity #2
Thoughts And Feelings

We must be aware of both thoughts and feelings.

Do you know the difference between thinking and feeling? If it sounds simple, be careful. The difference is like night and day. Yet people often get them confused.

This is an activity that helps the whole family learn the difference between thoughts and feelings. Place a box on a table. Pretend you can put anything in the world into that magic box. Think about something you want to put into the magic box, write it down on a slip of paper and put the paper in the box (each family member does this).

What each family member wrote is probably a thought. A thought is a product of thinking, which can be an idea, an opinion, a belief or an action.

Remove one piece of paper at a time from the magic box, asking each family member how he or she feels about what is written on each paper. Be sure your answers involve a feeling—not a thought. Sometimes it's hard to know what you are feeling. Each family member will have different feelings about each of the things in the magic box. Look at the following list of feeling words and choose one or two words which describe how you feel about each thing in the magic box. Think of other feeling words to add to the list:

comfortable	uncomfortable	confused
happy	sad	glad
unhappy	frustrated	fearful
angry	tired	delighted
worried	exhausted	devastated
concerned	lonely	stupid
wild	confident	scared
joyous	nervous	hungry
love	negative	positive
insecure	terrible	terrific
excited	defeated	unsure
energetic	satisfied	horrible

For each item in the box, each family member completes the following sentence (each person practices putting a feeling and a thought together):

I feel _____ about _____

(the item written on the piece of paper).

Doing this exercise teaches the difference between feelings and thoughts. Maybe you feel happy about having your favorite sports team in the box. Another family member may feel frustrated about the same sports team. Perhaps you feel scared about a spider that someone put in the box while another family member may feel delighted about it. You may feel comfortable about your child's friend who moved to another school; your child may feel sad and lonely about this friend. You may feel excited about the thousand dollars that someone else put in the magic box. The connections between your thoughts and feelings become evident as you experience this activity. A good listener (a person who is attentive to others) tries to hear both thoughts and feelings.

Sentence Completions

Each family member completes all five sentences. This activity works best when the sentences are written down. All family members take turns reading the first completed sentence, followed by each person reading subsequent ones.

1. Listening means _____

   _____

2. A good listener must_____

   _____

3. One of my favorite things to listen to in nature is _____
   because _____

4. One thing I need to practice that will help me become a better
   listener is _____

5. If people in my family were better listeners,_____

   _____

Children's Literature And The Arts

- Visit a library to find books that relate to *listening*. If you need help, ask a librarian. Read each book first to make sure you are comfortable with the contents.
- Be aware of music, television shows, movies and theatrical performances which provide special opportunities for talking to your child about *listening*.

Friendliness

During an interview about friendliness with a sixth grade class, a young lady said something in front of the entire class that I will never forget. One of her peers asked her, "Are you friendly to others in your home?" With tears rolling down her cheeks, she said, "I have been mistreating my mother for years. I can't wait to see my mother to give her a hug and start treating her like a friend."

Definitions and Thoughts

A person with a friendly nature generally shows kindness and good will toward others and expresses a cheerful attitude. People who are friendly treat others with warmth and affection and are willing to care about, share with and help others.

Friendliness is a *ValueSkill* that helps in creating better families, better classrooms, better communities, better work places and even a better world. Most of us think of a friend as someone we know, like and trust. Friendliness is a personal quality that allows us to consider another's feelings and to respond in the way we would like to be treated.

A friend:

- greets you in the morning,
- shares with you,
- hugs you even when you're not sad,
- smiles at you,
- is nice to you,
- spends time with you,
- gives you compliments,
- cares about you when you are hurt, and
- gives you the bigger piece of cake or the larger bowl of ice cream.

Friends sometimes:
- act unfriendly because they are having a bad day or something is bothering them,
- argue with one another but usually make up quickly,
- make things better between themselves by saying, "Let's cool down for awhile and talk about this later,"
- can feel lonely and left out of activities, and
- can hurt your feelings. It is important to let them know when this happens because many times they do not mean to be unfriendly.

While I believe in the importance of teaching children how to make and keep good friends, I feel it is also important to teach them how to interact with strangers. "Stranger danger" must be explained in a manner that creates caution—not fear, and precaution—not avoidance of strangers.

Benefits

Friendliness:
- makes a difficult task easier when someone offers assistance,
- makes our homes, classrooms and work places happier places to be,
- creates a positive environment as people share and care about each other,
- helps us feel that we are not alone,
- helps us feel like we belong,
- makes us feel happy and involved,
- allows us to share our ideas and dreams with others,
- gives us someone to talk to about important things, and
- gives us a chance to help others when they need help.

Mealtime Discussion Questions

Are most kids and adults friendly?

Why/why not?

Is it important to be friendly?

Why/why not?

Why do you think some people are unfriendly?

Do you ever find yourself becoming unfriendly when you are with someone who is unfriendly?

Why/why not?

Do you believe that most people want to be friendly?

Circle Time Topics
Focus On Personal Experiences

Have your family sit in a circle. When everyone is comfortable, a family member reads the first "circle time topic" below to the rest of the family. Each member takes a turn talking about a personal experience relating to the topic. Other family members ask clarifying questions (see Chapter Five). Your family can continue discussing the second and third "circle time topics" if time permits.

Discuss a time when:

* someone was friendly to you.
   a. How did you feel when this happened?
   b. How do you think the other person felt when they acted in a friendly manner?
* you felt badly because you were unfriendly to another person.
   a. How do you think you made the other person feel?
   b. What did you do after you acted unfriendly?
* you were friendly to another person.
   a. How did you feel during this time?
   b. How did the other person respond to your friendliness?

A Quick and Easy Family Project
A Mobile Of Friendliness

Cut paper into different geometric shapes, like circles, squares, diamonds and triangles that are about the same size.

Ask each family member to paste magazine pictures or pictures they've drawn representing friendliness onto the geometric shapes.

Make a family mobile about friendliness by suspending the shapes from a metal hanger with string.

Family Activity #1
Interview

Write each family member's name on an individual slip of paper. Fold all the slips of paper and put them in a bowl. Each family member chooses one slip of paper from the bowl to determine who he or she will personally interview. Use the questions below to guide the interviews. As each question is asked, write down the response. When all interviews are completed, each interviewer takes a turn telling the family what he or she learned about the other person during the interview. Friendships grow as you get to know each other better.

1. Your name: _____

2. Describe your family: _____

_____

3. Describe your childhood: _____

_____

_____

4. Favorites (books, desserts, songs, movies, colors, hobbies):

_____

_____

5. What values are important to you? _____

_____

6. Describe yourself in three words:_____

_____

7. Describe your school or job: _____

_____

_____

8. What do you like and dislike about your school or job?

_____

_____

9. What are your greatest accomplishments? _____

_____

_____

10. Describe something you hope to accomplish: _____

_____

_____

11. What wish do you have for the world? _____

_____

_____

12. Thank you. Do you have any questions you would like to ask me? _____

_____

_____

_____

Family Activity #2
Stories About Four Farmers

For this family activity, divide a large piece of paper into four equal sections. Label the sections Field A, Field B, Field C and Field D (see illustration below):

Field A	Field B
Field C	Field D

Farmer Number One's Story:

Farmer One was a stingy person. So Farmer One bought only six seeds of poor quality to plant.

In Field A, draw six poor quality plants that grew from six poor quality seeds.

Farmer Number Two's Story:

Farmer Two did not want to work very hard, but he was wise enough to know that he needed good quality seeds to grow healthy plants. So Farmer Two bought only six seeds of good quality to plant.

In Field B, draw six good quality plants that grew from six good quality seeds.

Farmer Number Three's Story:

Farmer Three decided to harvest a big crop but he was too stingy to spend the necessary amount of money. So Farmer Three bought 20 seeds of poor quality to plant.

In Field C, draw 20 poor quality plants that grew from 20 poor quality seeds.

Farmer Number Four's Story:

Farmer Four was a wise farmer. He learned a long time ago that whatever he puts into the soil is what he gets out of the soil. So Farmer Four bought 20 seeds of good quality to plant.

In Field D, draw 20 good quality plants that grew from 20 good quality seeds.

Discuss as a family the meaning of the story about the four farmers. All family members are asked to describe which farmer they would like to be and why.

If most of the seeds of friendship you plant today are of good quality (positive; honest; healthy; friendly; complimentary; kind;

open; cooperative; enthusiastic), then you are moving in the direction of becoming a good friend.

It is important to know that you can choose how you behave. Remember, you harvest what you sow!

Sentence Completions

Each family member completes all five sentences. This activity works best when the sentences are written down. All family members take turns reading the first completed sentence, followed by each person reading subsequent ones.

1. Friendliness is _____

2. I showed good will toward another person when _____

3. It is easiest to be friendly toward others when _____

4. It is hardest to be friendly toward others when _____

5. I believe the thing that most often causes unfriendliness between my friends and myself is _____

Children's Literature And The Arts

- Visit a library to find books that relate to *friendliness*. If you need help, ask a librarian. Read each book first to make sure you are comfortable with the contents.

- Be aware of music, television shows, movies and theatrical performances which provide special opportunities for talking to your child about *friendliness*.

Kindness

While driving home one night after visiting my oldest son at college, the car lights dimmed and then proceeded to go out completely. The night seemed particularly dark and the road was not well traveled. My two younger sons put their heads out of the car windows to help direct me as I drove along the road. Finally, we came upon a late night convenience store where we thought we might get help. A couple who had stopped to buy bread and milk offered to share their home for the night. To this day, our sons talk of the midnight snack, the comfortable lodging and the hearty breakfast we were served in the morning by those generous people.

Definitions and Thoughts

Kindness is acting toward others in a pleasant or sympathetic manner. It is a trait we associate with people who have a gentle nature and are generous, hospitable, thoughtful, charitable, understanding and goodhearted.

Kindness:
- is a way of showing good will,
- lets others know we care about them, and
- shows other people we respect them.

You can show kindness by:
- helping someone with chores,
- deciding to do what someone else wants to do instead of what you want to do,
- telling Mom or Dad how much you appreciate dinner,
- visiting a sick friend, neighbor or relative,
- lending someone a pen or pencil,
- sharing your lunch with a friend, and

- shoveling snow from the walk or driveway of an elderly neighbor.

Benefits

Kindness:

- helps us make and keep friends,
- makes our homes, schools and communities nicer places to live and work,
- helps others feel worthwhile,
- helps people stay healthy, and
- produces good neighbors.

Mealtime Discussion Questions

What things can you do to show kindness toward others?

Why is it important to be kind?

Is it sometimes difficult to be kind to others?
Why/why not?

Do you believe that most people are kind to each other?
Why/why not?

What would each home, classroom and community be like if everyone was kind to one another?

Circle Time Topics

Focus On Personal Experiences

Have your family sit in a circle. When everyone is comfortable, a family member reads the first "circle time topic" below to the rest of the family. Each member takes a turn talking about a personal experience relating to the topic. Other family members ask clarifying questions (see Chapter Five). Your family can continue discussing the second and third "circle time topics" if time permits.

Discuss a time when:

- someone was kind to you.

      a. What did the person do?

      b. How did you feel?

- someone was unkind to another person and you knew this was wrong.

      a. What did you do about it?

      b. Did either person know how you felt?

- you felt badly for someone and you did something kind for him or her.

      a. What did you do?

      b. How did you feel when you were showing kindness to this person?

A Quick and Easy Family Project
A Family Drawing About Kindness

Each family member has a piece of paper on which to draw things that illustrate kindness. The drawings can be scenes of people or animals being kind to one another, symbols that make you think of kindness, or promises from you for future acts of kindness. Proudly display your family drawings about kindness. They can be hung individually or you can put the drawings together to make a mural or wall hanging.

Family Activity #1
Role Playing Situations

Kindness is being gentle and goodhearted toward others. Whether a person acts kindly or unkindly does make a difference. The following role-playing situations are designed to look at the difference between a kind approach to life and an unkind approach to life.

I. Role playing situation: being unkind to someone by teasing
Choose The Players:

1. Tommy, the new neighbor, who is being teased and feels sad
2. Another kid(s) from the neighborhood who is teasing Tommy
Role Play The Situation:

> Tommy is a new kid in the neighborhood. After school, another kid(s) from the neighborhood begins teasing him.

Discussion:

> How did Tommy feel when he was teased? Why do some kids tease others? Do family members sometimes tease each other?

II. Role playing situation: being kind to someone who is being teased
Choose The Players:

1. Tommy, the new neighbor, who is being teased and feels sad
2 Another kid(s) from the neighborhood who is teasing Tommy
3. One or two members of Tommy's family who try to stop the teasing by helping the neighborhood kid(s) understand why it is wrong to tease (family members may need to play multiple roles in small families)
Role Play The Situation:

> It is after school and Tommy is again being teased. Tommy's family member(s) tries to stop the teasing.

Discussion:

> How did Tommy feel when someone from his family tried to help him? Is it difficult to try to stop people from teasing others? How can all of us help prevent teasing in our homes?

Family Activity #2:
15 Things We Do As A Family

Work together to make a list of the things you do as a family. List them on the following chart. Decide how each item relates to the four categories. Mark the appropriate box for each thing on the list.

- Place an "H" by each item you do while at home.
- Place a "P" by each item your family enjoys doing with people from outside your family.
- Place an "✳" by the five favorite things you do as a family.
- Place a "$" if doing the activity costs money.

15 Things We Do As A Family	H	P	✳	$
1.				
2.				
3.				
4.				
5.				
6.				
7.				
8.				
9.				
10.				
11.				
12.				
13.				
14.				
15.				

Sentence Completions

Each family member completes all five sentences. This activity works best when the sentences are written down. All family members take turns reading the first completed sentence, followed by each person reading subsequent ones.

1. Kindness toward others means_____
_____

2. When someone is kind to me I feel _____
   because _____
   _____

3. One of the most unkind things I have seen happen in school or at work is_____
_____

4. If my brother(s) or sister(s) or friend(s) showed more kindness toward me, _____
_____

5. I want my family members to be kind because _____
_____
_____

Children's Literature And The Arts

- Visit a library to find books that relate to *kindness*. If you need help, ask a librarian. Read each book first to make sure you are comfortable with the contents.
- Be aware of music, television shows, movies and theatrical performances which provide special opportunities for talking to your child about *kindness*.

Cooperation

My third son was eighteen months old when my family went to a picnic on a hot August day. He seemed fine when we left home, but at the picnic he became ill and developed a fever. Although he had experienced high fevers before, they were never anything like this one. Within minutes he was convulsing violently, became completely limp and started turning blue. He was having a febrile seizure—a seizure related to his high temperature. Everyone at the picnic tried to help. As I held my son, people guided me up the stairs to the bathroom where others filled the tub with cool water. I put him in the tub to reduce his fever. In the meantime, other people called an ambulance. Still others moved cars and directed traffic so the ambulance team had quick access. On that hot August day many people cooperated to help care for my son.

Definitions and Thoughts

Cooperation is working together to complete a task. It enables families to do many marvelous things. Cooperation is possible when there is good communication between people. When each person contributes, everything works more easily and efficiently. Today more than ever we need to work together to strengthen our families and our communities.

Cooperation means two or more people are working or playing together to achieve a goal.

Cooperation:

- is needed whenever two or more people work together,
- means being willing to combine efforts for success, and
- begins with each of us treating others as we like to be treated.

Benefits

Cooperation:
- helps us complete tasks more easily,
- allows each person to offer advice, ideas and encouragement,
- helps us work together to be more productive, and
- brings order and peace to our homes.

Mealtime Discussion Questions

Why is it important for people to learn to work together and play together agreeably?

What happens when people do not cooperate?

Why is it sometimes hard to cooperate?

How do we know what other people are feeling when we are working and playing with them?

Why is cooperation a positive goal for our family?

Circle Time Topics
Focus On Personal Experiences

Have your family sit in a circle. When everyone is comfortable, a family member reads the first "circle time topic" below to the rest of the family. Each member takes a turn talking about a personal experience relating to the topic. Other family members ask clarifying questions (see Chapter Five). Your family can continue discussing the second and third "circle time topics" if time permits.

Discuss a time when:
- you cooperated with many people in order to make something successful.
    - a. How many people were involved?
    - b. How did other people cooperate?
- you needed help to do something and someone helped you.
    - a. How did someone help you?
    - b. How did you feel when you received the help?

- you saw that someone needed help to do a job and you helped him or her.

  a. How did you help?

  b. How do you think the other person felt when you helped?

A Quick and Easy Family Project
The Machine

One family member begins this activity by pretending to be one "part" of a machine. This person might pretend to be a wheel by moving both arms in a circle, a valve by moving his or her body up and down, or a whistle by moving one arm and making the sound of a whistle.

A second family member joins the first person to become another part of the machine. Other family members become additional parts of the machine. (In small families, people can use different parts of their bodies to represent different parts of a machine.)

The goal is for the entire family to be creative in making a machine with multiple moving parts.

Some parts of a machine move, some do not. Some parts make noise, others do not. You might want to pretend to be more than one type of machine.

Good luck in building your machine. As you will see, it will take cooperation as piece-by-piece you build the machine.

Family Activity #1
A Family Cooperation Project

Since there are many projects that need to be done around the house, plan a family cooperation project. It might involve cleaning closets, cleaning the garage or working on the lawn together. Talk about what needs to be done, delegate duties and begin. The job will be done quickly because every member of the family has cooperated.

Family Activity #2
Chores And Responsibilities

One of the best ways for a family to cooperate is to share chores. Listed below are some family chores and responsibilities. Add any other tasks you might think of to this list:

wash the dishes	clean-up your bedroom
mow the lawn	make the beds
vacuum the house	fold the laundry
rake leaves	wax the car
shovel snow	wash the laundry
water plants	walk the pets
iron clothes	make home repairs
wash the car	brush the pets
prepare meals	empty the trash
paint the house	do the dusting
clean up by putting	clear the table
things away	after meals

Each family member chooses several things they are responsible for or will be responsible for doing at home. Make a chart listing each person's name and the chores and responsibilities each has chosen. Post the chart.

Sentence Completions

Each family member completes all five sentences. This activity works best when the sentences are written down. All family members take turns reading the first completed sentence, followed by each person reading subsequent ones.

1. Cooperation is _____

_____

_____

2. Our family cooperates by _____

    _____

3. I like to cooperate with _____

    _____

    _____

4. Families need to cooperate because _____

    _____

    _____

5. When people work together to get something done, _____

    _____

    _____

Children's Literature And The Arts

- Visit a library to find books that relate to *cooperation*. If you need help, ask a librarian. Read each book first to make sure you are comfortable with the contents.
- Be aware of music, television shows, movies and theatrical performances which provide special opportunities for talking to your child about *cooperation*.

Encouragement

A friend of mine tells this story: At the age of 7 his daughter suddenly developed an intense interest in baseball and registered to be on a Little League team. At that time there were only a few girls in the league. My friend remembers that the coach worked patiently to help her swing level, keep her eye on the ball and stay in the batter's box. "My wife and I went to each game to cheer for her even though she struck out each time at bat," he says. He thought she might go through the whole season and never get a hit or even get on base. All of the parents continued to cheer her on with "way to watch'em" and "nice try." "The day the ball hit her bat and she ran to first base while the crowd stood, clapped and cheered, still," he says, "sends chills up my spine." All of us at times have felt we might never get to first base. During such moments we could all use a crowd and a coach to cheer us on with encouragement.

Definitions and Thoughts

Encouragement can be described as inspiration, love, reassurance, support and belief in someone. Saying and doing encouraging things for others contributes to their self-confidence and courage when they are attempting new or difficult things.

Consider the difference between a family member who says "*I can't*" and one who says "*I can*" and "*I will.*" The power behind these words affects what a person actually does. It would be helpful if each time a child utters the words "*I don't think I can do it*" someone replies, "*I believe you can do it,*" "*Keep trying,*" or "*Don't give up!*"

Such statements encourage us to try to accomplish things we otherwise might not think of trying. As children attempt new things, it is important for them to know that they will not always be successful. Even the most distinguished inventors, scientists, writers, leaders and artists have faced failure and have made mistakes. But, through effort, hard work and practice, we learn about life and are better able to reach our goals.

Encouragement is an important factor in our lives. The support of others through encouragement opens doors and allows us to experience life more fully and with less fear.

Encouragement:

- teaches that trying is as important as achieving,
- reminds people that without trying, it is impossible to succeed,
- supports the idea that it is important to set goals and natural to make mistakes, and
- happens when we care about others and treat others in a special way.

Benefits

Encouragement:

- helps others feel more positive and try harder,
- lets others know their efforts are appreciated,
- opens the door for communication,
- supports a person's willingness to risk, and
- is a key to friendship, self-confidence, courage, success and happiness.

Mealtime Discussion Questions

Do you think it is important for people to be encouraging to others? Why/why not?

Do your classmates or co-workers encourage you to do better and try harder in school or work? Why/why not?

How do you encourage others (advise; care; help; cheer; listen; love; support)?

Do you believe it is possible for your family members to help each other feel more positive about themselves?

What would your family be like if members encouraged each other to do their best?

Circle Time Topic
Focus On Personal Experiences

Have your family sit in a circle. When everyone is comfortable, a family member reads the first "circle time topic" below to the rest of the family. Each member takes a turn talking about a personal experience relating to the topic. Other family members ask clarifying questions (if necessary, see Chapter Five). Your family can continue discussing the second and third "circle time topics" if time permits.

Discuss a time when:

- you needed encouragement and someone encouraged you.
    a. Why did you need encouragement?
    b. How did this person give you encouragement?
- you saw someone needing encouragement and you didn't do anything about it.
    a. What was happening to this person?
    b. What stopped you from giving this person encouragement?
- a friend needed encouragement and you provided it.
    a. What do you think your friend was feeling?
    b. What did you do to provide encouragement?

A Quick and Easy Family Project
Encouragement Creations

Using various materials like paper, fabric, cardboard, markers, string, large safety pins and glue, family members make individual encouragement badges or signs for themselves. Be creative. Wear them or put them in a prominent place as daily reminders. The following examples are phrases you might use on your encouragement creations:

I can do it!

Give it your best effort!

We can do it together!

You can count on me!

I will do it!

Try-try-try !

You can do it!

We can do it!

Don't give up!

Believe in yourself!

I believe in me!

One day at a time!

Examples of encouragement creations:

Family Activity #1
A Short Story About Encouragement
Write a short story about encouragement. Each person helps to create the story by contributing to the tale. One member volunteers to record what each person says. It is sometimes fun to build the story by taking turns adding one sentence at a time. Stories can take unexpected twists and turns. Your challenge is to incorporate the theme of encouragement into your story. When you finish the story, read it aloud.

Family Activity #2
Bookmarks For Encouragement
Each family member will make a bookmark for another family member. Pick names from a hat to be sure that each person gets a bookmark. Decorate the bookmarks as you like and write encouraging statements on them. You can refer to the list of encouraging statements in *A Quick and Easy Family Project.* Bookmarks can also be made for other friends or relatives. Laminate the bookmarks if you want to make them more durable.

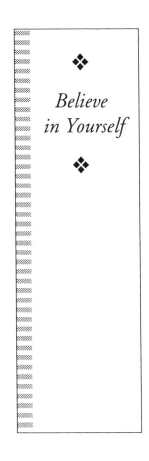

❖

Believe in Yourself

❖

Sentence Completions

Each family member completes all five sentences. This activity works best when the sentences are written down. All family members take turns reading the first completed sentence, followed by each person reading subsequent ones.

1. Encouragement is _____

_____

2. I think some people do not encourage others because _____

_____

_____

3. Others give me encouragement when _____

_____

_____

4. One way I encourage my friends is _____

_____

_____

5. Encouragement can help my family members become _____

_____

_____

Children's Literature And The Arts

- Visit a library to find books that relate to *encouragement*. If you need help, ask a librarian. Read each book first to make sure you are comfortable with the contents.
- Be aware of music, television shows, movies and theatrical performances which provide special opportunities for talking to your child about *encouragement*.

Honesty (with Kindness)

I was perplexed when my son displayed in his bedroom a math paper of his that bore a red 'F'. He was a junior in a very competitive high school and had always done quite well academically. Why would he display a failing paper in his bedroom? His answer both astonished and, in a different sort of way, pleased me. He said, "Sometimes I don't like my school. It should have been obvious to the teacher that some of my friends got 'A's' because they cheated by getting a copy of the test early. I refused to look at the test when it was offered to me, so I'm proud of my 'F'. I earned it honestly." I was proud of it too!

Definitions and Thoughts

Honesty is being honorable and fair in one's behavior. It means being truthful and open about what one says to another person.

Honesty begins with parents. Children learn what they see modeled each day in their homes.

Honesty with kindness stresses the importance of telling the truth without purposely hurting others. Whether we our dealing with a sales person who has given us the wrong change, someone on the phone who is trying to sell us aluminum siding, or a friend we don't want to see at a particular time, we need to deal with them in an honest and kind manner.

Honesty with kindness:
- is a quality that allows people to trust each other,
- should apply to how we think about and treat ourselves,
- allows us to tell others what we really feel without embarrassing them or hurting their feelings, and
- requires that people do what they say they will do.

Benefits

Honesty:

- allows us to earn the trust and respect of others,
- causes others to trust what we say,
- builds lasting friendships,
- brings a sense of well being to a home, and
- makes our communities, schools and homes happier and safer places.

Mealtime Discussion Questions

Why is it important for family members to be honest with each other?

Why are people in our society dishonest?

Why is it important to express our feelings to others?

Why is "honesty with kindness" such an important combination?

Do you believe that people are usually honest with kindness?

Circle Time Topics

Focus On Personal Experiences

Have your family sit in a circle. When everyone is comfortable, a family member reads the first "circle time topic" below to the rest of the family. Each member takes a turn talking about a personal experience relating to the topic. Other family members ask clarifying questions (see Chapter Five). Your family can continue discussing the second and third "circle time topics" if time permits.

Discuss a time when:

- someone's honesty caused you to like and trust them.
  a. What was the situation?
  b. How did you know he or she was being honest?
- you told the truth even though it was hard to do.
  a. What caused you to tell the truth?
  b. How did you feel about being honest in this situation?

- someone lied to you.
    - a. What were the circumstances?
    - b. How did you feel when someone lied to you?

A Quick and Easy Family Project
Skits On Honesty

Your family is to create and act out several skits about honesty. For example, set up a situation in which someone at school or work is wearing unusual looking clothes. Another member of the family acts out the role of someone being honest without kindness, telling the person that the clothes look ridiculous. Then someone acts out a scenario by making comments on the outfit honestly, but with kindness. Think of other situations that can be portrayed using both approaches and have family members act them out.

Family Activity #1
Word Hunt

H
O
N
E
S
T
Y

Using the seven letters in the word HONESTY, try to find at least 25 hidden words. You can use the seven letters only once in each new word. Be sure to give each person an opportunity to participate in the activity. One person records the words as they are discovered.

For a greater challenge, use the 19 letters in the words HONESTY WITH KINDNESS to see how many hidden words you can find.

Family Activity #2
Preferences

Honesty is telling others truthfully what you think and feel about an issue. One family member reads aloud the ten questions below, as well as the possible answers provided. Each person chooses an answer for each of the ten questions and records them on a sheet of paper. Discuss each family member's choices. Another way to do this activity is for individual family members to verbalize an answer after each of the questions and possible responses have been read aloud. Discuss the family members' responses.

1. What season do you enjoy the most?
   -Spring   -Fall
   -Summer -Winter
2. Which would you rather be?
   -rich and happy
   -happy and famous
   -famous and rich
3. Which is worse?
   -to be ignored by your friends
   -to be rejected by your friends
   -to be ridiculed by your friends
4. Which chore do you like doing the least?
   -vacuuming the house
   -washing the dishes
   -cleaning up the house
5. What would you rather do on a warm summer afternoon?
   -hike in the woods
   -swim in a lake
   -go to a movie
6. Which would you prefer to do?

-go to art class
-go to gym class
-go to music class

7. What would you like to do if you received $100?
   -save it all
   -spend it all
   -spend $50 and save $50
8. Which color is your favorite?
   -blue   -yellow   -orange
   -green   -red   -purple
9. What would bother you the most?
   -when a friend teases you
   -when a friend tattles on you
   -when a friend gossips about you
10. Where would you rather go?
    -to a museum
    -to a planetarium
    -to a library

Sentence Completions

Each family member completes all five sentences. This activity works best when the sentences are written down. All family members take turns reading the first completed sentence, followed by each person reading subsequent ones.

1. Honesty with kindness means _____
   _____

2. It is not always easy to be honest because _____
   _____

3. One way to be honest with kindness is _____
   _____

4. Stealing is _____ because

_____

5. If people in our community were more honest _____

_____

Children's Literature And The Arts

- Visit a library to find books that relate to *honesty*. If you need help, ask a librarian. Read each book first to make sure you are comfortable with the contents.
- Be aware of music, television shows, movies and theatrical performances which provide special opportunities for talking to your child about *honesty*.

Patience

My courageous and tenacious sister has multiple sclerosis. She lives in an old monastery which has been converted into a wheelchair-accessible home. According to the residents, most of the nurse's aides are thoughtful and dedicated individuals who care about the needs and comfort of the residents. Witnessing the patience that is required of these aides as they minister to the needs of the residents, I appreciate their willingness to take however long is needed to bring comfort and care to each individual. I am also impressed with the patience of the residents, when many times each day their needs are not met as quickly or thoroughly as they would like. So many of us seem to be in a hurry, demanding instant service. It seems that many of us have lost the quality of patience.

Definitions and Thoughts

Patience is the ability to remain calm, to be understanding and to be tolerant during times of difficulty. It is a necessary quality for maintaining good health in a stress-filled society.

Patience:
- allows us to think before acting or responding,
- is a skill that allows us to experience beauty and joy in life because of a relaxed attitude, and
- involves tolerance and understanding.

Benefits

Patience:
- helps us wait for something we want,
- allows us to wait peacefully for things to happen,
- helps us be more tolerant of others,

- helps us refrain from complaining when we are feeling annoyed,
- prevents us from being overbearing and demanding,
- helps us deal with stress, and
- gives us time to reflect on what is important.

Mealtime Discussion Questions

Do you believe that patience is an important quality to have? Why/why not?

Would you say that most people you know are patient or impatient?

When is it most difficult for you to be patient?

Can you recall anyone in history or anyone recently in the news who demonstrated patience?

Can you think of jobs which demand patience? Explain.

Circle Time Topics

Focus On Personal Experiences

Have your family sit in a circle. When everyone is comfortable, a family member reads the first "circle time topic" below to the rest of the family. Each member takes a turn talking about a personal experience relating to the topic. Other family members ask clarifying questions (see Chapter Five). Your family can continue discussing the second and third "circle time topics" if time permits.

Discuss a time when:

- a teasing remark or put-down made you lose patience.
  - a. How did you lose patience?
  - b. How could you control yourself during such times?
- you stayed calm in a difficult situation.
  - a. What was the situation?
  - b. What were the benefits of remaining patient?
- you felt totally relaxed.
  - a. Were you at home or away from home?

b. How often do you feel this relaxed?

A Quick and Easy Family Project
Find An Object

Family members choose individual objects at home that remind them of the quality of patience. Each family member shows his or her object to the rest of the family and explains why it makes him or her think about patience.

Family Activity #1
Dealing With Patience

1. Each family member thinks of situations which bring about impatient feelings. Here are a few examples of typical situations which cause people to feel impatient:

Situation #1: You can't find your assignment or project and you are late for school or work.

Situation #2: Your ride to a birthday party or to a special meeting is late.

Situation #3: You are hungry, but can't find anything you really like to eat in your house.

Situation #4: Your classmates or colleagues are teasing you.

Situation #5: Your friend is not sharing.

Situation #6: You're watching a special TV program and the TV becomes blurry.

Situation #7: You are struggling with complicated instructions to assemble something.

Situation #8: You are on your way to an appointment and you might be late because of rush-hour traffic.

2. Consider and write situations on a piece of paper that cause each family member to feel impatient:

Name_____ Situation _____

Name_____ Situation _____

Name_____ Situation _____

Name_____ Situation _____

Name_____ Situation _____

3. Listed below are ideas that can help us be more patient. Take turns reading them aloud:

    a. Talk about the situation with someone.

    b. Find something else to do and return to the problem later.

    c. Take turns.

    d. STOP! Consider a new option and try it.

    e. Explain your feelings to the person with whom you are impatient, and tell him or her what you need.

    f. Ask to talk to the person in charge.

    g. Accept the other person's choice.

    h. Ignore the situation.

    i. Ask someone to help you with what you are trying to do.

    j. Flip a coin.

    k. Ask someone for advice.

    l. Remember that "this too shall pass."

    m. Count to 10, take a deep breath and relax.

    n. Plan a strategy to deal with the issue that is frustrating you.

    o. See a counselor.

    p. Understand that it often takes more time than we expect for things to happen.

4. All family members identify which ideas will help them deal effectively with the frustrating situations they wrote down. If none of the ideas above seem like they will work, think of other solutions.

Family Activity #2
An Interview About Patience

One family member is selected to be interviewed by the rest of the family (grandparents, friends or other relatives can also be interviewed). Take turns asking the following questions. Feel free to ask the person being interviewed clarifying questions (see Chapter Five).

Interview questions:

1. What does patience mean to you?
2. Are you a patient person? When/when not?
3. What is your favorite toy or activity? Does this help you develop more patience? Why/why not?
4. What two words best describe you? Are these words associated with patience or impatience?
5. Describe two things you enjoy doing that help you feel relaxed.
6. Do you want to become more patient? Why/why not?
7. If you want to be more patient, how can you achieve this goal?
8. Who do you think is the most patient person you know?
9. Do you think your family members need to become more patient?
10. If you think your family needs to become more patient, what general suggestions would you offer?

Sentence Completions

Each family member completes all five sentences. This activity works best when the sentences are written down. All family members take turns reading the first completed sentence, followed by each person reading subsequent ones.

1. Patience is _____

   _____

2. I know I need more patience when_____

   _____

3. The most difficult time for me to be patient is _____

_____

4. Patience is difficult for many people because _____

_____

5. The time when I am most relaxed is _____

_____

Children's Literature And The Arts

- Visit a library to find books that relate to *patience.* If you need help, ask a librarian. Read each book first to make sure you are comfortable with the contents.
- Be aware of music, television shows, movies and theatrical performances which provide special opportunities for talking to your child about *patience.*

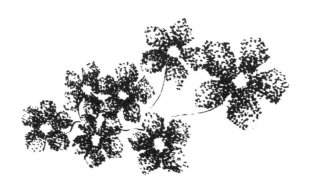

The seven ValueSkills II are:

being considerate,

being courteous,

being respectful of property,

being responsible for personal care,

being self-confident,

being enthusiastic

and being courageous.

Chapter Ten

Family Activities for Teaching ValueSkills® II

This chapter presents the second group of *ValueSkills* discussed in *Loving Is Natural, Parenting Is Not.* The seven *ValueSkills II* include:

consideration

courtesy

respect for property

responsibility for personal care

self-confidence

enthusiasm

courage

I have been teaching *ValueSkills* since 1972. During the first ten years I taught them to elementary age children in small counseling groups. In 1982, I developed a curriculum entitled *Classroom Super Teams,* based on *ValueSkills,* which consists of teacher guides, student workbooks and illustrated story boards. Since that time I have acted as a *ValueSkills* coach and teacher, working with entire classrooms.

I found that discussing *ValueSkills* with an entire class is significantly more effective in bringing about positive change than talking with individuals or only part of a class. Consider a situation where one classmate bullies others and those being bullied silently struggle alone to defend themselves. Now, consider what happens after a whole class discusses what it means to be a bully. The people being picked on now feel supported and more self-confident. It becomes very difficult for the bully to continue behaving badly toward others.

Exploring *ValueSkills* with the entire family works the same way. Together, families develop attitudes and skills that truly bring about support and teamwork.

As we explore the information and activities provided in this chapter, we continue to build the foundation for healthy character development. Our children continue to internalize values as they learn about *ValueSkills II*. Our goals include developing awareness of *ValueSkills* and using them in our daily lives.

Below is a review of safeguards and guidelines to use during family activities:

Safeguards

1. Do not discuss things that might embarrass other family members.
2. What family members say must be respected and held in confidence (do not talk to others about family discussions).
3. Each family member always has the right to "pass" (to say nothing if he or she so chooses).
4. *Treat others the way you want to be treated.*

As A Family . . .

- define each *ValueSkill* and talk about why it is important,
- use the activities provided, including *Mealtime Discussion Questions, Circle Time Topics, Quick and Easy Family Projects,*

Family Activities and *Sentence Completions* to introduce and teach *ValueSkills,*
- encourage each other to practice *ValueSkills* and congratulate each other for putting *ValueSkills* into action,
- select books, music, movies and artistic performances to share that provide opportunities for talking about each *ValueSkill,*
- post on the family message board the *ValueSkills* which are being discussed and practiced, and
- look for real life events or people that illustrate *ValueSkills* in action or being ignored.

Continue to build a family team by getting together twice a week for 20 to 30 minutes to discuss *ValueSkills* and participate in the *ValueSkills* activities. Family relationships improve and harmony increases as each person internalizes and acts upon *ValueSkills.* Individuals discover they are creating positive images of themselves with other family members as they spend this time together.

ValueSkills® *II Family Activities* are presented on the following pages.

Consideration

*Our school nurse has a delightful nine year-old son.
When he was four, he became disabled as the result of
an accident caused by a drunk driver. This young man
asked each of his classmates to spend one day in a wheelchair so they could better understand what he experiences.
The students then exchanged letters. The school nurse's
son wrote, "Life in a wheelchair is aggravating sometimes.
I don't let it get to me. Everyday I get more independent.
Before the accident, I never thought I would lose my legs.
I would never have said that I was glad to have my legs.
The lesson (of the experience using a wheelchair) was
not only to help you see what it is like to be in a wheelchair, but also to tell you that you never know the value
of something until you lose it." His classmates wrote letters
expressing the frustration, fear, loneliness and discomfort
they felt being in a wheelchair for just one day. They talked
about being ignored, teased and treated rudely. This was
a time when a group of students gained a new awareness
of people with disabilities and, in turn, greater respect
and consideration for a determined and sensitive classmate.*

Definitions and Thoughts

Consideration means being thoughtful or sympathetic to another
person. Being considerate shows concern for another person's circumstances and feelings. It means being aware of another person's
needs and doing something for that person. Consideration is
demonstrating good manners.

Consideration:

- of another person is an outward sign of respect and care,
- implies trying to avoid doing annoying things to others
  and trying to avoid hurting other people's feelings, and

name of his or her friend.

Family Activity #2
Service Projects For Your Family

Service projects provide assistance to others and teach consideration for others. This activity gives each family member an opportunity to do something special for another person or group of people.

Doing things for others brings about feelings of satisfaction and accomplishment. Each person can choose an individual project or the family can work on one project together. Listed below are suggestions for service projects. Think of other things you can do:

- pick up litter in a park
- baby-sit for someone
- help someone with a task (writing a letter; reading the newspaper; cooking a meal; mowing the lawn; shoveling the driveway)
- work for a day at a soup kitchen
- feed a pet for someone who is on vacation
- tutor someone without charging money
- organize a group of people to donate their time at a nursing home
- volunteer to help someone who is handicapped
- clean graffiti off the wall of a community building
- check on the well-being of an elderly neighbor

Service Project Contract

Name(s) _____

Date _____

Title of Project _____

Description of Project

_____

_____

_____

_____

When, Where, How Long

_____

_____

_____

_____

Evaluation

_____

_____

_____

_____

Sentence Completions

Each family member completes all five sentences. This activity works best when the sentences are written down. All family members take turns reading the first completed sentence, followed by each person reading subsequent ones.

1. Consideration means _____

   _____

2. A friend shows consideration when _____

   _____

3. People are inconsiderate when _____

   _____

4. The idea of having everyone in our family become more considerate is _____

   _____

5. I wish that everyone in my family _____

   _____

Children's Literature And The Arts

- Visit a library to find books that relate to *consideration*. If you need help, ask a librarian. Read each book first to make sure you are comfortable with the contents.
- Be aware of music, television shows, movies and theatrical performances which provide special opportunities for talking to your child about *consideration*.

Courtesy

I work with a school principal who practices courtesy when working with students, parents and staff. While treating others with dignity, he listens to all sides of a concern and then honestly and kindly expresses his views. He uses ValueSkills as part of his school-wide discipline approach, and in fact personally introduces ValueSkills to all of the middle school students. I have often heard him say, "This is what we expect from each other." "Tell me your side of the story." "What ValueSkill(s) did you break?" "I care about you but I don't like what you did." "Can you self-correct and treat others the way you want to be treated?" "I want you to tell me what you are going to do to be more courteous." His idea of courtesy truly reflects the first eight ValueSkills: listening, friendliness, kindness, cooperation, encouragement, honesty with kindness, patience and consideration.

Definitions and Thoughts

Courtesy means being polite and having good manners. It means acting in a manner that does not embarrass other people. Courtesy shows a belief that every person has dignity and worth.

Courtesy:

- is a common standard of behavior showing that a person knows how to behave politely toward others, and
- involves saying things like "*please,*" "*thank you*" and "*excuse me.*"

Benefits

Courtesy:

- shows respect for others,
- causes others to feel respected,

- brings order to our homes, and
- makes our homes pleasant places to live.

Mealtime Discussion Questions

What are some examples of courteous behavior?

Why is it important to act in a courteous manner when you are away from home? When you are at home?

Can you think of a time when you observed someone being discourteous?

Why are people sometimes rude and discourteous?

Do you believe that people are generally courteous? In schools? In restaurants? In work places?

Circle Time Topics
Focus On Personal Experiences

Have your family sit in a circle. When everyone is comfortable, a family member reads the first "circle time topic" below to the rest of the family. Each member takes a turn talking about a personal experience relating to the topic. Other family members ask clarifying questions (see Chapter Five). Your family can continue discussing the second and third "circle time topics" if time permits.

Discuss a time when:

- you noticed someone saying "*please*" and "*thank you*" to others.
  - a. Where were you?
  - b. What were the reactions of the other people?
- someone was rude to you.
  - a. How did this make you feel?
  - b. Why do you think this person was rude?
- you were rude to another person.
  - a. How did it make you feel?
  - b. How else could you have responded?

A Quick and Easy Family Project
A Short Story

Write a short story about courtesy. Each person helps write the story by taking turns contributing. One family member records what each person says so the story can be read later. The family can tell a story about how a discourteous family changes into a courteous family or about a family that is never courteous.

Family Activity #1
The Prize

Think about an appropriate and affordable family prize that can be shared at the end of this activity. The prize could include visiting an amusement park, going out for dinner, renting a movie, having a pizza party, making a favorite dinner together, visiting the zoo or the museum, going to the park for a picnic or going on a hike.

To earn the prize, your family (as a team) must earn 20 points. These points will be earned over a period of time. Each time someone "catches" another person being courteous and records the courtesy on a designated sheet of paper, the family gets one point. After the family earns 20 points, they earn the prize. Spend time together talking about the ways people were courteous to each other.

Family Activities #2
The Family Appreciation Chain

When family members appreciate each other, they usually are more courteous toward each other.

What do you appreciate about your family? What things about your family are you thankful for?

Begin this activity by making ten 1" by 8 1/2" slips of paper for each family member. For example, if there are three people in your family you will make 30 slips.

Every day for five consecutive days, each family member writes two new things they appreciate about an individual family member or about the entire family on individual slips of paper.

After five days, everyone reads their appreciations to the family. When all the appreciations have been read, make a continuous "appreciation chain" by forming circle links with the slips of paper and interlocking them one after another. Use staples to keep each link in place. After all the links have been added, hang the chain as a reminder of your family's importance.

Sentence Completions

Each family member completes all five sentences. This activity works best when the sentences are written down. All family members take turns reading the first completed sentence, followed by each person reading subsequent ones.

1. Courtesy means _____

_____

2. Being courteous is important because _____

_____

3. Two ways I can show courtesy in my home are_____

and _____

4. I believe that most people are/are not courteous in our community because _____

_____

5. I wish my family showed more courtesy _____

_____

Children's Literature And The Arts

- Visit a library to find books that relate to *courtesy*. If you need help, ask a librarian. Read each book first to make sure you are comfortable with the contents.
- Be aware of music, television shows, movies and theatrical performances which provide special opportunities for talking to your child about *courtesy*.

Respect for Property

One of my students was caught vandalizing a school bus seat with a knife. Concerned and embarrassed, the boy's parents talked with him before a meeting the following morning in the principal's office. They discussed vandalism and its effect on the community. They agreed that the boy would be honest about what he did and work to pay for repairing the damage. The principal listened as this young man admitted his role in the incident. He explained that although he and two other boys had cut the seat, he personally had not taken the knife to school. The principal agreed to accept the boy's offer to pay for the repairs, thanked him for his honesty and never demanded that he tattle on his peers. The other boys chose not to admit what they had done. This student learned a lot that day. He learned that he must respect the property of others, that he must be willing to work to repair what he damages and that others sometimes are not willing to tell the truth. He also learned that admitting the mistake and working toward correcting it earned respect from others. His parents were not happy, but they realized that their son had learned several important lessons.

Definitions and Thoughts

Respect for property involves understanding the value of the things you own, as well as objects and real estate owned by others. It means taking care of your own property and insures that you will not purposely damage or destroy things that belongs to others.

Respect for Property:
- means you throw trash in a proper receptacle rather than out of the car window or in someone's yard,
- means you hang up and care for your clothes,
- means putting things away when you are done using them, and
- means appreciating the value of things.

Benefits

Respect for Property:
- saves time, energy and money that would otherwise be spent replacing or fixing damaged items,
- keeps things looking nice and working well, and
- creates an awareness that everyone is responsible for preserving the environment.

Mealtime Discussion Questions

Do you believe that most people respect the property of others? Why/why not?

Why do you think people destroy things that belong to others?

Is vandalism a problem in your school, workplace and community? Give an example.

Do you believe that your friends have pride in their belongings, and in their school, workplace and community? Why/why not?

Give examples of how people show they have pride in their homes, schools, workplaces and communities.

Circle Time Topics
Focus On Personal Experiences

Have your family sit in a circle. When everyone is comfortable, a family member reads the first "circle time topic" below to the rest of the family. Each member takes a turn talking about a personal experience relating to the topic. Other family members ask clarifying questions (see Chapter Five). Your family can continue discussing the second and third "circle time topics" if time permits.

Discuss a time when:

- you saw someone breaking things, destroying property or littering.
    a. Where were you?
    b. How did you feel when you saw this?
- something that was special to you was broken, destroyed, or stolen.
    a. How did it happen?
    b. What did you do when this happened?
- you planned ways to take better care of your toys, books, sports and recreational things, clothes, furniture or home.
    a. What plans did you make?
    b. Did you follow through with your plans. If you did, are you continuing to follow through?

A Quick and Easy Family Project
Respecting Personal Things

All of us have belongings that are special to us; we take special care not to harm or damage them. It is important to respect and appreciate those things that family members say are important to them. By taking care of other people's property, we show respect for them also.

1. Each family member chooses four things that are valuable to him or her.
2. Each person lists the things that he or she has chosen.
3. Each person takes a turn telling why these things are valuable.
4. Discuss ways family members can show respect for each other's personal things.

Family Activity #1
Tender Loving Care

Families acquire many things as time goes by. Personal property needs to be maintained. But often we don't find the time to do necessary repairs and up keep. As a family, look around your home for things that need "tender loving care." Choose a few projects to do, plan your approach and do the projects together.

Family Activity # 2
Creating A Comfortable Living Space

In this activity your family works as a group to brainstorm one or two changes in your home that would bring more comfort and relaxation to family members.

Listed below are questions to begin the discussion:

1. Are there ways to rearrange your home for better useability?
2. How could you make your home more comfortable?
3. Do you have a place to relax?
4. Does each family member have a personal space?
5. Is there a place in your home to listen to music? . . . to read? . . . to play a board game? . . . to enjoy a conversation with others?

After your family has discussed various ways to create a more comfortable, relaxing and usable home environment, decide what changes you want to make. Develop a plan and make the changes.

Sentence Completions

Each family member completes all five sentences. This activity works best when the sentences are written down. All family members take turns reading the first completed sentence, followed by each person reading subsequent ones.

1. Respect for property means_____

_____

2. Vandalism means _____

_____

3. A favorite possession that I would not want to have ruined or broken is _____

_____

4. I wish our family took better care of_____
because _____

_____

5. Respect for property is important to our family because ___

_____

_____

Children's Literature And The Arts

- Visit a library to find books that relate to *respect for property.* If you need help, ask a librarian. Read each book first to make sure you are comfortable with the contents.
- Be aware of music, television shows, movies and theatrical performances which provide special opportunities for talking to your child about *respect for property.*

Responsibility for Personal Care

As a counselor, I listened thoughtfully as Billy told me how all of his classmates laughed at him, pushed him around and ignored him on the playground. This was not the first time Billy had been in my office crying. He felt hated and discouraged. I asked him if he wanted me to talk to the other kids in his classroom. With tears in his eyes, he said yes. But he did not want to be there when I spoke to them. As I gathered his classmates in a circle, a few of the ring-leaders laughed, trying to make light of the situation. But most of the students listened attentively, then openly and tenderly spoke to the issue of personal care. They told me that Billy was not taking good care of his body. "He smells," announced one little girl. "He never washes his hair, his hands or his face," said another. Others were upset by his eating habits. They all thought Billy needed help. We discussed how to be honest with kindness when talking to Billy about our concerns. We focused on how to communicate with others regarding sensitive issues. A few students thought that the school nurse could help Billy develop a plan for his own personal hygiene. We decided to invite her to class so that all the students could benefit from her advice. I asked the school nurse to work privately with Billy after each lesson. Then I met with Billy to discuss the concerns expressed by his classmates. During the next few weeks we turned our focus to "treating others the way we want to be treated." Over the course of the year, Billy's appearance gradually improved. He began playing with others on the playground. This experience not only provided each student with an opportunity to think about his or her own personal care, but it also taught a group of students about the nuances of dealing with sensitive issues.

Definitions and Thoughts

Physical care deals with taking responsibility for the well-being of one's body. It involves personal hygiene and grooming, as well as attention to diet, exercise and health care.

Personal care:

- improves one's self-image,
- involves cleanliness,
- involves exercise which tones muscles and relieves stress,
- involves eating nutritious foods, and
- eliminates abuse of tobacco, drugs and alcohol.

Benefits

Personal care:

- results in better health,
- generates positive feelings about oneself,
- helps individuals make more friends because their appearance is more attractive, and
- develops self-confidence.

Mealtime Discussion Questions

Do you believe that it is important to keep your body clean? Why/why not?

What are good eating habits?

Why is exercise important? What are some ways you can exercise?

How do you feel about smoking, the use of alcohol and the use of illegal drugs?

How does physical care affect friendships?

Circle Time Topics

Focus On Personal Experiences

Have your family sit in a circle. When everyone is comfortable, a family member reads the first "circle time topic" below to the rest

167

of the family. Each member takes a turn talking about a personal experience relating to the topic. Other family members ask clarifying questions (see Chapter Five). Your family can continue discussing the second and third "circle time topics" if time permits.

Discuss a time when:

• you were involved in regular exercise.
  a. How often did you do this activity?
  b. Why was this particular activity enjoyable to you?
• you thought about doing something to improve your physical care but did not do it.
  a. Do you believe that you will do it?
  b. Do you need someone to help you accomplish it?
• you did something relating to physical care that was helpful to you.
  a. Did it involve eating, exercising, keeping clean or something else.
  b. Did you do it everyday?

A Quick and Easy Family Project
A Family Personal Care Activity

As a family, do something together that expresses respect for personal care such as: taking a walk or hike, making a healthy meal, reading about nutrition and planning a week-long healthy menu for the family or participating in a sports activity.

Family Activity #1
A Family Journal on Physical Care

Writing a journal gives you an opportunity to express your family's thoughts, feelings, experiences and reactions about something. This activity involves writing about taking care of your body. You might include 1) favorite family foods and the need for nutritious foods, 2) the need for exercise and each family member's exercise of choice,

3) the importance of a physical check-up and the last time each person had one, 4) caring for your teeth and the last time each person visited the dentist, 5) how each family member relaxes, 6) the dangers of tobacco, alcohol and other drugs, and 7) dressing appropriately.

Family Activity #2
Circles

Our bodies are like engines. We need to take care of them just as we take care of our cars or they will break down. Make a list of ten things we do to take care of ourselves.

Draw ten different size circles on separate sheets of paper (small to large) and cut them out. In each circle, write one of the things from the list you have made. Attempt to prioritize the ten things and write the more important ones on the bigger circles. Make a small hole at the top and bottom of each circle. Use string to tie the circles together from large to small to make a vertical hanging. Hang it in a special spot.

Sentence Completion

Each family member completes all five sentences. This activity works best when the sentences are written down. All family members take turns reading the first completed sentence, followed by each person reading subsequent ones.

1. Physical care is _____

_____

2. I believe that physical care is important because _____

_____

_____

3. My favorite way to get exercise is _____

_____

4. One example of a good eating habit is _____

_____

_____

5. One thing I believe about personal care is _____

_____

_____

Children's Literature And The Arts

- Visit a library to find books that relate to being *responsible for personal care*. If you need help, ask a librarian. Read each book first to make sure you are comfortable with the contents.
- Be aware of music, television shows, movies and theatrical performances which provide special opportunities for talking to your child about being *responsible for personal care*.

Self-confidence

I have three terrific yet very different sons. For each one of them, I was a Little League Baseball coach. As a coach I had four rules: everyone plays, everyone gets to play different positions, everyone tries to do their best and everyone has fun. We had great times and most parents appreciated this philosophy. Our win/loss record was not nearly as important as having each player contribute his/her best effort to the team. I did not fully appreciate the effect this supportive coaching approach had on the players until years later, when a mother asked me if I remembered her son. "Even though he never got a base hit," she said, "he always looked forward to the games and to your encouragement. He had fun and his skills improved a little with each game. His self-confidence soared that year. Thank you." This mother reminded me that self-confidence can be enhanced or diminished by significant people in our lives.

Definitions and Thoughts

Self-confidence is believing in yourself. It is trusting your thoughts and your feelings. It is based on how you feel about yourself—worthy or unworthy, smart or stupid, friendly or unfriendly, adequate or inadequate. Self-confidence is learned from significant people such as parents, siblings, teachers and friends.

Self-confidence:

- is acquired over the years, mostly learned from others and derived from actions,
- does not mean you are conceited,
- is acquired by focusing initially on the things you do right, looking at areas that need improvement, then working on

those areas,

- results from working hard to accomplish a goal, and
- means not letting others make you feel inadequate or unimportant.

Benefits

Self-confidence:

- causes a person to act in a responsible manner,
- helps a person do what he or she thinks is right,
- helps a person say "no" when necessary,
- helps a person tackle and achieve difficult tasks, and
- gives a person the courage to do what he or she believes is the right thing to do.

Mealtime Discussion Questions

Do you believe that every person has worth and should be treated with dignity? Why/why not?

What helps people feel more self-confident?

What can you do to feel more self-confident?

How do you disregard others' remarks when they are putting you down, teasing you, or calling you names?

What would happen in your home if the number one goal was helping others acquire a more positive self-image?

Circle Time Topics

Focus On Personal Experiences

Have your family sit in a circle. When everyone is comfortable, a family member reads the first "circle time topic" below to the rest of the family. Each member takes a turn talking about a personal experience relating to the topic. Other family members ask clarifying questions (see Chapter Five). Your family can continue discussing the second and third "circle time topics" if time permits.

Discuss a time when:

- another person said or did something to boost your self-confidence.
  - a. What did the person do?
  - b. How did this help you feel more self-confident?
- you did something that made you feel self-confident.
  - a. Did it take a long time to learn how to do it?
  - b. Do you plan to continue to do it?
- you thought about things you like about yourself.
  - a. Does your family know you have these qualities?
  - b. How long have you liked these things about yourself?

A Quick and Easy Family Project
Skits About Self-confidence

Create short skits about self-confidence and have your family act them out. (You may choose to use props.) Think about challenging situations that people face in life, such as trying out for a play, asking for a raise or telling a teacher or a boss that you disagree with his or her decision. Choose a situation to act out. In the skit, family members give encouragement to the person who is facing the difficult situation. The goal is to help the person gain self-confidence in facing the challenge. As a family, discuss the powerful effects of receiving encouraging support. Choose other situations to act out.

Family Activity #1
The Family Coat Of Arms

You are a member of the ingenious and marvelous human race.
You are an important person.
Never let anyone make you feel inadequate or unworthy.
Whatever you give to others you really are giving to yourself.
You need to take time to focus on good things about yourself
  and your family.

173

Directions for completing the "Family Self-confidence Coat of Arms" are listed below:

- Draw a Coat of Arms on a large piece of paper (see sample at the end of this activity).
- Write the names of all your family members in the top ribbon-like section.
- The six main areas in the body of the coat of arms will be used to represent each of the six topics listed below. Use symbols, drawings and words to represent one topic in each area, illustrating "positive and meaningful" things about your family:
  1. Family sports and hobbies
  2. Family relatives and friends
  3. Family favorites
  4. A symbol to describe each family member
  5. Our family's favorite vacation(s)
  6. A family dream
- Write four words to describe positive characteristics about your family in the top four side border sections of the coat of arms.
- Write a saying, a motto or a wish about your family in the bottom border section of the coat of arms.

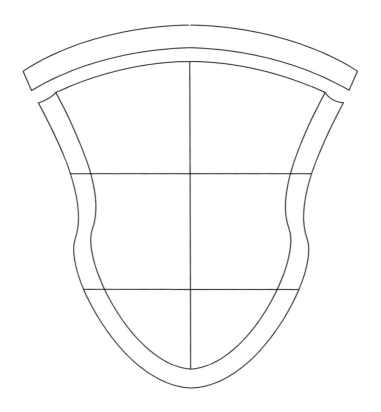

Family Activity #2
Self-confidence Builders

The chart below identifies six things that help individual family members build self-confidence. Make a chart like the one shown.

In the boxes after each of the six self-confidence builder topics, write the names of the family members who GIVE self-confidence to others by doing the things listed on the left-hand side of the chart.

This activity is an opportunity to say, "Thanks" to the person(s) in your family who contributes to the self-confidence of others. Identify other things your family members do to build family self-confidence and add them to the chart.

Self-confidence Builders	
Taking care of family clothing	
Being kind to each other	
Keeping our home neat and clean	
Encouraging others	
Sharing things with others	
Being patient with others	

Sentence Completions

Each family member completes all five sentences. This activity works best when the sentences are written down. All family members take turns reading the first completed sentence, followed by each person reading subsequent ones.

1. Self-confidence is _____

_____

2. Two people who I believe give me support to enhance my self-confidence are _____

_____

3. I help others become more self-confident when _____

_____

4. The more I believe in myself _____

_____

5. My self-confidence is _____

_____

Children's Literature And The Arts

- Visit a library to find books that relate to *self-confidence*. If you need help, ask a librarian. Read each book first to make sure you are comfortable with the contents.
- Be aware of music, television shows, movies and theatrical performances which provide special opportunities for talking to your child about *self-confidence*.

Enthusiasm

When I consider the meaning of enthusiasm I am reminded of a photograph of one of my sons. As a young child he periodically became quite sick. I took him from doctor to doctor, yet over those early years he continued to have problems with his health. At age three he became dehydrated and had to be hospitalized. For two weeks no one could determine what was wrong. Finally a pediatric specialist determined the cause, and my son was operated on immediately. His condition quickly improved. I still smile at the picture of him eating solid food for the first time in three weeks. Seeing the joy in his eyes as he devoured a hamburger with great enthusiasm was a priceless gift.

Definitions and Thoughts

Enthusiasm is being excited about something. Enthusiasm is having zest for living. It makes us think about the gifts we have and helps us strive for those things that are meaningful in life. People who focus on the good in life and take time to enjoy each day are more enthusiastic.

Enthusiasm:

- makes us eager to do things,
- adds richness and excitement to our lives,
- increases our awareness of those things that can give us a fuller life,
- helps us enjoy life's treasures, and
- is an important factor in acquiring a positive attitude.

Benefits

Enthusiasm:

- makes us feel ambitious and alive,
- is contagious,
- overshadows negative attitudes,
- inspires others,
- adds a spark of joy to a task, and
- fosters creativity.

Mealtime Discussion Questions

Do you sometimes feel enthusiastic or excited about things? When? Where? What?

Why is feeling enthusiastic important?

Do you believe most people focus on positive or negative things in their lives? Why?

What are some things you appreciate?

What can you do to help yourself, your friends and your family feel more enthusiastic?

Circle Time Topics

Focus On Personal Experiences

Have your family sit in a circle. When everyone is comfortable, a family member reads the first "circle time topic" below to the rest of the family. Each member takes a turn talking about a personal experience relating to the topic. Other family members ask clarifying questions (see Chapter Five). Your family can continue discussing the second and third "circle time topics" if time permits.

Discuss a time when:

- something you did, appreciated or believed made you feel terrific and enthusiastic.
  - a. How often do you feel enthusiastic about this activity, thing or belief?

      b. Do you usually feel enthusiastic?
- something caused you to feel a lack of enthusiasm toward school or work.
       a. Why did you feel this way?
       b. What did you do about it?
- someone did something for you that made you feel enthusiastic.
       a. How many people were involved?
       b. Did this feeling last for a long time?

A Quick and Easy Family Project
Life Appreciations

As a family, take turns finding the 40 things listed in the following puzzle grid. Talk about what our lives would be like if we did not have these things. The answers to the puzzle grid are located on page 183.

air	animals	appliances
birds	books	butterflies
charity	computer	democracy
desserts	education	entertainment
exercise	family	feelings
flowers	food	freedom
friends	health	hobby
joy	laughter	learning
love	medicine	mountains
nature	newspapers	rainbow
religion	school	senses
sports	sunshine	technology
television	travel	trees
water		

Life Appreciation Puzzle Grid

Q	T	B	S	E	N	S	E	S	K	W	S	B	H	W
N	E	W	S	P	A	P	E	R	S	R	P	U	Y	A
U	L	X	T	R	E	E	S	T	E	O	O	T	B	T
D	E	S	S	E	R	T	S	W	S	W	R	T	I	E
M	V	A	A	B	T	C	O	M	P	U	T	E	R	R
A	I	R	T	K	S	L	L	D	K	W	S	R	D	T
B	S	H	H	H	F	H	O	B	B	Y	P	F	S	E
O	I	E	Q	F	O	P	T	M	C	L	E	L	D	C
O	O	A	R	R	O	V	J	O	Y	C	Y	I	L	H
K	N	L	L	E	D	L	A	U	G	H	T	E	R	N
S	E	T	I	E	L	B	P	N	J	A	N	S	Z	O
E	S	H	Z	D	X	I	J	T	J	R	A	U	Z	L
N	C	L	K	O	C	B	G	A	B	I	T	G	F	O
T	M	D	E	M	O	F	O	I	F	T	U	F	E	G
E	D	U	C	A	T	I	O	N	O	Y	R	Q	E	Y
R	O	D	I	U	R	R	S	X	N	E	D	L	N
T	U	B	Q	S	U	N	S	H	I	N	E	E	I	F
A	N	I	M	A	L	S	I	Q	C	L	X	M	N	R
I	H	C	V	P	R	A	I	N	B	O	W	O	G	I
N	E	F	A	M	I	L	Y	G	G	V	T	C	S	E
M	E	D	I	C	I	N	E	E	A	E	G	R	R	N
E	X	E	R	C	I	S	E	A	G	Y	I	A	M	D
N	N	V	V	Z	A	P	P	L	I	A	N	C	E	S
T	R	A	V	E	L	S	C	H	O	O	L	Y	M	N

Family Activity #1
A Container Of Enthusiasm

Cover the surface of a heavy cardboard container or box (such as an Oatmeal box) to make a decorative container. Using newspapers and magazines, tear or cut out words and pictures that express or symbolize enthusiasm. Torn edges look more interesting than cut edges.

Glue the pictures and words over the entire surface of the container. While you are doing this, talk about why you chose these particular images and words. When the container is totally covered, allow the glue to dry. Then, using a brush, carefully apply a coat of white glue that has been thinned with water (one-half glue to one-half water) over the entire surface of the container. Do not over-wet the words and pictures. Apply several more coats of thinned glue to protect the surface, allowing each coat to dry before applying the next coat.

Family Activity #2
Our Family Graffiti Board

Having a sense of humor can make the difference between a dull, unfulfilling life and one of joy and enthusiasm. We sometimes take life so seriously that we forget to laugh. Being able to laugh, have fun, enjoy nonsense and, at times, act silly is part of what keeps us healthy.

This family activity involves making a "fun-loving graffiti board." Draw or create your own jokes, riddles, sayings and cartoons and find amusing jokes and cartoons in print that can be cut out. Paste them on a stiff board. The board can be cut into an interesting shape. Choose humor that is funny and kind to others.

You might want to consult your local library or ask friends for suggestions. Find "healthy" humor, be creative and enjoy the experience.

Solution to the Life Appreciation Puzzle Grid from page 181

	T		S	E	N	S	E	S			S	B		W
N	E	W	S	P	A	P	E	R	S	R	P	U		A
	L		T	R	E	E	S		E		O	T	B	T
D	E	S	S	E	R	T	S	W			R	T	I	E
	V				C	O	M	P	U	T	E	R	R	
A	I	R			L					S	R	D	T	
B	S	H		F	H	O	B	B	Y		F	S	E	
O	I	E	F	O		M				L		C		
O	O	A	R	R	O		J	O	Y	C		I		H
K	N	L	E	D	L	A	U	G	H	T	E	R	N	
S		T	E	L		N		A	N	S		O		
E	H	D	I	T	R	A		L						
N	L	O	G	A	I	T	F	O						
T	E	M	I	T	U	E	G							
E	D	U	C	A	T	I	O	N	O	Y	R	E	Y	
R		R	S	N	E	D	L							
T	S	U	N	S	H	I	N	E	E	I	F			
A	N	I	M	A	L	S	I	L	M	N	R			
I	R	A	I	N	B	O	W	O	G	I				
N	F	A	M	I	L	Y	G	V	C	S	E			
M	E	D	I	C	I	N	E	E	R	N				
E	X	E	R	C	I	S	E	A	D					
N	A	P	P	L	I	A	N	C	E	S				
T	R	A	V	E	L	S	C	H	O	O	L	Y		

Sentence Completions

Each family member completes all five sentences. This activity works best when the sentences are written down. All family members take turns reading the first completed sentence, followed by each person reading subsequent ones.

1. Enthusiasm is _____

   _____

2. I get excited when I _____

   _____

3. I would be more enthusiastic if I had the courage to _____

   _____

   _____

4. I believe that sometimes people are not enthusiastic because

   _____

   _____

5. The kids in my school or the people in my work place would be more enthusiastic if _____

   _____

Children's Literature And The Arts

- Visit a library to find books that relate to *enthusiasm*. If you need help, ask a librarian. Read each book first to make sure you are comfortable with the contents.
- Be aware of music, television shows, movies and theatrical performances which provide special opportunities for talking to your child about *enthusiasm*.

Courage

As a counselor in a senior high school, one of my respon-sibilities was to help college bound students prepare their college applications. One young woman revealed her unique perspective on courage in her essay. "I learned about laughter last summer," she wrote. "Not the laughter I had become accustomed to, but the laughter of life. For one week, I lived, worked, played and prayed with more than one hundred cancer patients, ages seven to seventeen, at Camp Good Days and Special Times. This camp offers a carefree, six day adventure for children afflicted with cancer. Each day brought new experiences, new joys and new problems. Each camper taught me much about life, and especially about the meaning of courage. Courage, I learned, is Tina, a young girl confined to a wheelchair completing a rope climbing course. Courage is Michelle, who has only one leg, but doesn't shy away from swimming or horseback riding. Courage is Ricky, legally blind yet always showing a smile that brightened my day. Thanks to these kids, I now have a new understanding about courage, about laughter, about love and about life."

Definitions and Thoughts

Courage is being brave enough to do what you believe is the right thing. Courage is being brave enough to face a difficult situa-tion. It is doing what you think is good for you, for others and for the community. Courage is saying "no" to someone who challenges you to do a dangerous thing. Courage means not being foolish enough to try a dangerous stunt.

Courage:
- is willingness to stand up for what you believe,
- is having the inner strength to withstand danger, fear or difficulty, and
- is inspired in us when we see courageous acts being done by others.

Benefits

Courage:
- helps us take control of our lives and choose what is best,
- helps us complete difficult tasks and ask for help, when necessary, and
- can be contagious when one person is willing to risk doing what he or she believes is right.

Mealtime Discussion Questions

What is the difference between being courageous by taking a stand or facing a difficult situation and being foolish by doing a dangerous stunt?

Does it take courage to stand up for a friend who is being picked on by others? Why/why not?

What are some things kids and parents do which require courage?

Why does it often take courage to do what you think is right?

How do you get courage?

Circle Time Topics

Focus On Personal Experiences

Have your family sit in a circle. When everyone is comfortable, a family member reads the first "circle time topic" below to the rest of the family. Each member takes a turn talking about a personal experience relating to the topic. Other family members ask clarifying questions (see Chapter Five). Your family can continue discussing the second and third "circle time topics" if time permits.

Discuss a time when:

- you saw someone have the courage to take a stand.
  - a. How did you feel about this person?
  - b. Do you have the courage to say "*no*" when others are saying "*yes*"?
- you had the courage to stand up for someone.
  - a. What made you take a stand?
  - b. How did the person you stood up for respond?
- you had the courage to face something that made you feel uncomfortable or afraid.
  - a. What did you have to face?
  - b. How did you find the courage to face the problem?

A Quick and Easy Family Project
Pictures Or Paragraphs About Courage

Members of the family draw individual pictures of themselves or write a paragraph depicting themselves acting in a courageous manner. After all family members have shared their pictures or paragraphs, display them in a prominent spot.

Family Activity #1
Flower Petals

Courage comes from within each of us. The courage to do what we think is right involves having the strength to face difficult problems without backing away or ignoring them. The better we feel about ourselves, the more courage we have to do the right thing.

Using the diagram on the following page as a guide, draw a large flower on a large sheet of paper: Write your family name in the center circle. Work together to fill each flower petal with the information requested:

Petal One: Write each person's favorite color on this petal.

Petal Two: Write a *ValueSkill(s)* that causes you to think of each individual in your family on this petal (example: Dad – considerate).

Petal Three: List ways family members want to be treated by others on this petal (example: Mother – with love and respect).

Petals Four and Five: List statements about courage made by individual family members. Begin the statements with, "*I want to have more courage to _____.*"

Petals Six and Seven: Think of a special quality for each family member. Write each person's name, the quality and an animal that has this same quality in these petals (examples: Cole – a spirited deer; Chris – a strong majestic lion; Jared – a lovable bear).

Petals Eight and Nine: Think of positive aspects of each member of your family. Choose forms of nature that are symbolic of these positive aspects. Write the person's name, the positive aspect and the form of nature representing each person in these petals (examples: Casidhe – a colorful rainbow; Terri – a radiant sunset; Christopher – a sun providing a warm, special glow).

Family Activity #2
Badge Of Courage

- It takes courage to admit shortcomings.
- It takes courage to lose weight by resisting that cupcake at a birthday party.
- It takes courage to stand up for yourself.
- It takes courage to be friends with a person who may not be popular with others.
- It takes courage to say "*yes*" when others say "*no*," and "*no*" when others say "*yes*."
- Courage means being free to be yourself and doing what you think is good for you and for others.
- All of the people in your family have courage. They need only to find it and act upon it.

To remember that you have courage, make a badge that commemorates the discovery of courage within yourself. Use materials found around the house such as paper, cardboard, wood, fabric, crayons, markers, string and glue. Each person chooses patterns and words to use on his or her personal Badge of Courage. Examples of possible badge shapes are shown below:

Examples of words of courage:
I have courage!   *Courage is contagious!*
Courage is in me!   *Taking a stand is courageous!*

Sentence Completions

Each family member completes all five sentences. This activity works best when the sentences are written down. All family members take turns reading the first completed sentence, followed by each person reading subsequent ones.

1. Courage is_____

   _____

2. I'm glad I have the courage to_____

   _____

3. I wish I had the courage to_____

   _____

4. Doing something dangerous because someone "dares you to do it" is _____

   _____

5. If more people had courage _____

   _____

Children's Literature And The Arts

- Visit a library to find books that relate to *courage*. If you need help, ask a librarian. Read each book first to make sure you are comfortable with the contents.
- Be aware of music, television shows, movies and theatrical performances which provide special opportunities for talking to your child about *courage*.

Summary

This completes the 14 *ValueSkills* family activities sections. All of these activities can be used over and over again as children grow and experience new life situations. Using the ideas presented throughout this book and practicing the 14 *ValueSkills* will have a significant effect on the amount of peace and joy your family experiences together. They will help build loving relationships and greater intimacy between family members. Through positive interactions you will record positive images in the hearts of those you love.

Loving Is Natural, Parenting Is Not: creating a value-centered family is a total approach to parenting designed to be referred to throughout your parenting career.

Glossary

A good citizen: A person who demonstrates participation in good faith in the affairs of one's community and country.

Apologizing: Saying, "*I'm sorry*," when appropriate.

Appropriate attention: Taking the time to listen to another person; spending quality time with someone; acknowledging good deeds; seeing the humor in life.

Appropriate responses: Being respectful and encouraging to others; sharing your feelings and thoughts honestly; increasing positive talk.

Boundaries: The limits a parent sets when determining what behaviors are acceptable and unacceptable; boundaries should be clear, fair, consistent, appropriate and reasonable.

Calmness: The absence of agitation and excitement; quietness, gentleness and peacefulness; calmness is necessary for effective communication.

Character: One's moral qualities and guiding principles.

Character development: Identifying, modeling and teaching inner qualities (basic common values) for encouraging moral strength.

Cheerleading: Being enthusiastic and upbeat; having a positive attitude; offering positive comments; applauding good effort.

Clarifying questions: Keeping the focus on the speaker; questions asked to help the speaker think more deeply about a topic.

Communication skills: Listening, asking clarifying questions, sending direct messages, giving validating statements, giving self-affirming statements and making direct command statements.

Compromise: Exploring options and working together to find an alternative when agreement cannot be reached.

Consequences: The effects of one's behavior; consequences can occur naturally, through *cause and effect*, or can be generated by parents or other authorities; they should be *appropriate and reasonable.*

Consideration: A *ValueSkill* defined as being thoughtful or sympathetic to another person's circumstances and feelings.

Cooperation: A *ValueSkill* defined as two or more people working together to complete a task.

Courage: A *ValueSkill* defined as being brave enough to do what one believes is the right thing, or being brave enough to face a difficult situation.

Courtesy: A *ValueSkill* defined as being polite; having good manners.

Direct command statements: Letting others know that you are concerned (safety issues) and/or, upset (behavior issues), and expect immediate and cooperative action from them.

Direct messages: Feelings and thoughts stated clearly and briefly; a feeling message, an encouraging message, a wonder message.

Discipline: An essential element of family life that informs children of parental expectations regarding behavior through teaching and modeling and provides appropriate consequences for misbehaviors.

Discipline with Calmness and Dignity: A four-stage approach to discipline; includes teaching, talking and problem-solving with children and seeking support from others outside the home when necessary.

Discretion: The quality of making prudent and wise decisions and choices.

Due process: The quality of providing equal application of the law and a fair hearing to all members of society.

Encouragement: A *ValueSkill* defined as inspiring others, loving others, reassuring others, supporting others and believing in others.

Encouraging: Focusing on a person's positive traits, acknowledging a person's strengths, recognizing a person's improvements and expressing appreciation for a person's efforts.

Encouraging messages: Direct messages that focus on another person's positive traits, strengths, improvements and efforts.

Endurance: The quality of being patient and persistent; having the courage and inner strength to continue.

Enthusiasm: A *ValueSkill* defined as being excited about something; having zest for life.

Explaining clearly and briefly: Expressing one feeling, one thought and one statement about what you need from the other person without nagging, lecturing or talkathons.

Express feelings constructively: Communicating with others without blaming and name-calling; keeping the focus on how one personally feels about a situation.

Feeling messages: Statements that tell what one is feeling and why; "*I feel* _____ *because* _____."

Friendliness: A *ValueSkill* defined as showing kindness and good will toward others; expressing a cheerful attitude; treating others with warmth and affection.

Goal-setting: Developing and evaluating a plan for accomplishing an individual or family goal.

Good will: The quality of finding goodness in people and in life.

Honesty (with Kindness): A *ValueSkill* defined as being honorable and fair; being truthful and open about what one says to another person.

Ignoring: When a person doesn't respond or pay attention to another person.

Internalization of a value: The process of accepting a value to the degree that it becomes part of one's value system; this occurs when one becomes aware of a value, uses it on one's own without prompting from others, feels emotional satisfaction when using the value, begins to use the value often and finally is committed to use it consistently; a value that has become an integral part of one's character; a value that has been thoroughly explored and is held in great esteem.

Interrupting: When a person speaks or makes noise as someone else is speaking.

Justice: The quality of being fair and equitable toward ourselves and others.

Kindness: A *ValueSkill* defined as acting toward others in a pleasant or sympathetic manner.

Listening: A *ValueSkill* defined as sitting quietly with ears open and mouth shut; looking at the person who is speaking, showing interest in what the person is saying and seeking to understand what is being said.

Live in the present: Focusing on and living fully in the moment.

Loyalty: The quality of maintaining one's obligations and commitments to those with whom one has relationships.

Love children unconditionally: Loving a child even though his/her behaviors are unacceptable.

Modeling: Setting an example by living the values that one wants to teach to children.

Moral character: Demonstrating integrity, honor and high principles.

Moral strength: The quality of acting upon that which is ethical in order to maintain the principles of humanity.

Parenting: Loving, nurturing, supporting and guiding children.

Parenting challenges: Loving children unconditionally, expressing feelings constructively, living in the present, setting boundaries and making character development a priority.

Parenting skills: Ten basic behaviors—stay calm, listen, encourage, use *ValueSkills*®, give appropriate attention, give appropriate responses, explain, allow for compromise, allow for consequences and apologize.

Patience: A *ValueSkill* defined as remaining calm, being understanding and tolerant during times of difficulty.

Praise: A verbal response connoting approval; technique that judges behavior as "good."

Principle of Reciprocity: What you need from me, I need from you.

Problem-solving: The third stage of *Discipline with Calmness and Dignity;* involves families working together to resolve concerns; includes defining a problem, asking clarifying questions, identifying three to five possible solutions, trying one of them and reporting the results.

Promoting ValueSkills: Finding opportunities to observe, discuss and teach the 14 *ValueSkills.*

Punishment: Used by parents to discourage unacceptable behavior; often involves a penalty or loss of privilege.

Respect for others: A trust that every human being has worth and deserves to be treated with dignity.

Respect for property: A *ValueSkill* defined as treating the things you own and the possessions of others with care and consideration.

Responsibility: Demonstrating accountability for one's behaviors and duties.

Responsibility for personal care: A *ValueSkill* defined as taking responsibility for the well-being of one's body; involves personal hygiene and grooming, as well as attention to diet, exercise and health care.

Reward: A tangible gift that tells the recipient his or her behavior is "good."

Safeguards: Rules for families to follow when doing *ValueSkills* activities; they include not embarrassing others, respecting what others say, allowing others the right to pass and following "*The Golden Rule.*"

Seeking additional support: The fourth stage of *Discipline with Calmness and Dignity* involves getting outside help when one's family is not functioning effectively; can be as simple as visiting a friend or relative for advice or as comprehensive as consulting a team of specialists.

Self-affirming statements: Clear and positive messages about oneself stated honestly to oneself.

Self-confidence: A *ValueSkill* defined as believing in yourself; trusting your thoughts and your feelings.

Self-control: The quality of seeking balance in one's life; of being "in control" of one's behavior.

Self-reliance: The quality of having the self-confidence and courage to give one's best effort in completing tasks and solving problems.

Synergy: Combining the energy and knowledge of two or more people to reach a common goal.

Talking: The second stage of *Discipline with Calmness and Dignity;* involves discussing a child's misbehavior, exploring why it happened, identifying more appropriate ways to handle the situation and re-teaching the *ValueSkill(s)* that relates to the unacceptable behavior; the child is an inextricable part of this process.

Teaching: The first stage of *Discipline with Calmness and Dignity;* telling children about the benefits and significance of one's values; *ValueSkills* activities are helpful resources for teaching values.

Team-building skills: Promoting, modeling, cheerleading, giving unconditional love and goal-setting; these skills build family cohesiveness.

The Golden Rule: Treat others the way you want to be treated.

Trust: The quality of believing in others who demonstrate a sense of honor and integrity.

Validating statements: Positive, heart-felt messages given freely and honestly by one person to another.

Values: Internal beliefs.

Value creation: See "Internalization of a value".

Values complex: An internalized set of interconnected values and virtues; constitutes one's entire internal value system; a person acts with greater respect and responsibility and is a more committed and dedicated citizen when he or she has a strong, healthy values complex.

ValueSkills: Essential, common inner strengths; basic character traits (values) that can be identified, taught and modeled (skills), and that serve as the foundation for developing moral character.

ValueSkills I: Includes listening, friendliness, kindness, cooperation, encouragement, honesty (with kindness) and patience.

ValueSkills II: Includes consideration, courtesy, respect for property, responsibility for personal care, self-confidence, enthusiasm and courage.

Virtues: Qualities of character that guide each of us to respond and choose in an honorable manner, even when we have no audience.

Wonder messages: Questions used to address difficult issues and uncomfortable situations; *"I wonder _____ ?"*

Index

A Child Who… 87
Apologizing 42
Appropriate attention 37
Appropriate responses 38
As A Parent, I Will Remember… 89-90

Boundaries 4

Calmness 30-31, 33, 53, 66
Character 5, 20, 27
Cheerleading 35, 44-45
Clarifying questions 55
Communication skills 49-63
Compromise 40
Consequences 41, 81-83
Consideration 150-155
Cooperation 123-127
Courage 185-190
Courtesy 156-160

Dignity 66
Direct command statements 62-63
Direct messages 56-58
Discipline with Calmness and Dignity 65-68, 75-86

Encouragement 35, 128-133
Encouraging messages 57
Enthusiasm 178-184
Explain 39
Express feelings constructively 3

Feeling messages 56-57
Friendliness 108-116

Goal-setting 45-47
Good citizenship 24

Honesty with kindness.. 134-139

I Mean What I Say 83-84
Ignoring.. 51
Interrupting.. 52

Kindness 117-122

Listening.. 34, 54, 102-107
Live in the present.. 4
Love children unconditionally 2, 45

Modeling.. 44

Parenting challenges .... 2 - 5
Parenting Checklist 91-95
Parenting skills 31-42
Patience.. 140-145
Praise 65-73
Principle of Reciprocity.. 77
Problem-solving 79-85
Promoting 44
Punishment.. 65-73

Respect for property.. 161-165
Respectful.. 24

Responsibility for personal care 166-170
Reward 65-73

Safeguards 99, 148
Seeking additional support 85-86
Self-affirming statements 60-61
Self-confidence 171-177
Stranger Danger 19, 109
Synergy 44

Talking 77-79
Teaching 76-77
Team-building skills 43-47
The Golden Rule 5, 19, 77

Validating statements 59
Value creation 19-20
Values .... ii, 17
Values complex 24
ValueSkills 16-27, 36, 97-146, 147-191
ValueSkills I 17, 21, 22, 23, 97-101
ValueSkills II 17, 22, 23, 147-149
Virtues 24-27

Wonder messages 57-58
Why We Stopped Teaching Values 7-13
   1950s 7-8, 13
   1960s 8-9, 13
   1970s 8-10, 13
   1980s 10-11, 13
   1990s 11-13

Ordering Information

Single Copy:

Order through your local bookstore or send a check for $14.95 (New York State residents add $1.20 for sales tax) plus $3 for shipping and handling to:

Coleman Press
SAN: 298-9492
Att: Order Department
P.O. Box 92339
Rochester, N.Y. 14692
Telephone/Fax: 716-242-0688

Multiple Copy Discounts:

To order larger quantities with multiple copy discounts – write, call or fax Coleman Press for information.

View the Gockley's Internet Home Page at
http://www.frontiernet.net/~gockley

Learn about *Gockley Associates, LLC,*
an organization dedicated to
bringing Character Education to families,
schools and the workplace, offering presentations
and seminars facilitated by the Gockleys.

Gockley Associates, LLC
awareness/prevention/renewal

About The Authors

Gil received Ed.M. and Ed.D. degrees from the University of Rochester in Guidance and Counseling in 1969 and 1973, respectively, and a C.A.S. degree from S.U.N.Y. Brockport in Educational Administration in 1977. He is celebrating his thirtieth year as an educator. Gil has worked as an elementary school teacher, counselor/guidance specialist (elementary, middle and secondary schools), assistant college professor (undergraduate and graduate levels), central office administrator and state/national consultant/presenter and writer in the areas of life/career education, parenting, family and character education.

Tanya received a B.S. degree from S.U.N.Y. Brockport in K-6 Elementary Education and Studio Art in 1972 and a M.S. degree from Nazareth College of Rochester in Elementary Education and Art Education in 1983. Since 1966, Tanya has worked as a studio artist, teacher, interior designer and writer.

Gil and Tanya are the co-founders of *Gockley Associates, LLC,* a corporation dedicated to the development and implementation of character education for families, schools and the workplace.

Gil and Tanya offer presentations and seminars and co-facilitate couples' groups. Use the Gockley's Internet Home Page (http://www.frontiernet.net/~gockley) to learn more about their organization. They are happily married, have three terrific grown sons and two delightful grandchildren.